QUICK PREP

Navigating the Criminal Trial Process

What You Need to Know

Kevin McKain

For additional copies or customer service inquiries, please e-mail west.customer.service@thomson.com.

ISBN 978-0-314-29397-8

Mat #41840406

DEDICATION

For my wife, Stephanie, who I only hope knows that everything I do is for her and our three beautiful children, Presley, Maddon and Charley.

For my parents, Joseph and Sandra, for always encouraging me to write–I use Dad's hardcover *Webster's Dictionary* to this day.

CONTENTS

Foreword

Six hours had now passed since the jury entered their twelve-by-twelve-foot room to begin deliberating the fate of my client. By now, John and I had walked, together and separately, several miles on the black marble floors of the Monroe County Courthouse in Rochester, New York. It was 3:45 p.m., and I knew that, unless the judge felt the jury was close to reaching a verdict, the jury would be let go at 4:30. Budget restraints now dictated that judges shut down their courtrooms at 4:30 to avoid having to pay staff and sheriff deputies overtime.

Fourteen months ago, John was arrested and charged with manslaughter in the first degree after he struck a man over the head with a broken beer bottle during a bar fight. John did not start the fight. In fact, he was at the bar with two of his best friends to celebrate their latest softball win when one of his friends got into an argument with another patron. The patron eventually threw a punch, and a full-blown bar fight ensued. At some point, John hit the man with the beer bottle. The man John struck went to the hospital with a concussion and died the following day as the result of an aneurism.

John was the last guy you would ever expect to be in this position. He had never been arrested before. His last traffic ticket for speeding was over ten years ago. He was forty-two years old. He had a job he enjoyed and that paid enough to allow his wife of eight years to stay home with his two boys, ages three and four. Yes, John was as nondescript as they came. But nondescript or not, John now faced five to twenty-five years in prison for manslaughter, a violent class B felony.

I got up to walk to the bathroom, leaving John on the bench near the locked courtroom door. Every time I left the courtroom, I carried my mobile phone in my hand, nervous that I might miss a call from the judge's secretary. When a jury begins deliberations, the judge's secretary takes the attorneys' mobile phone numbers so they can be reached when the jury reaches a verdict or has a question. Any time the jury has a question or requests testimony to be read back, the attorneys must return to the courtroom. During a typical jury's deliberations, I expect at least a couple of calls for those purposes. Due to that knowledge, my phone becomes like an electrical shock device in the hands of a torture expert. Everywhere I walk, I am conscious of the fact that, at any time, my phone might signal me to the news that the jury has reached a verdict, or it could just be my wife reminding me to pick up milk before I come home.

When I return to the bench, John sits still, staring intently at the white lines dissecting the marble floors. By this time, there is very little I can say to him to assuage his fears, including the most primal of fears: losing one's freedom. John's wife, Sara, was somewhere else in the labyrinth of the courthouse, likely staring intently at some other section of the floor. In her purse, she held onto John's wallet, watch, and wedding ring, the things he would not be allowed to take with him if the jury returned a guilty verdict, and the court deputies were forced to put handcuffs around his wrists. It is fortunate he has a wife who can hold onto these things. My office is littered with items entrusted to me by clients who had no one else to take possession of the items when their time came.

Ten months ago, John was offered a plea deal by the prosecutor that would have guaranteed that he serve two years in prison. I remember sitting in my office with John and Sara to explain the terms of the offer. We discussed what could happen if he rejected the offer and what I thought the chances were of getting through a trial unscathed. I remember taking a long sip of my coffee when I heard the question I most dislike having to answer: What should I do? I explained to John that I could not tell him what he should do. All I could do was provide him with as much information as I could so he could make that difficult decision. When John and Sara left my office that day, John had already decided he would not accept the offer. Twenty-four hours later, I relayed his answer to the court and the assistant district attorney handling the case, and I began preparing for the trial that had culminated with awaiting the jury's verdict.

At ten after four, I felt the familiar buzz in my suit jacket pocket. I pulled my phone from my pocket and instantly recognized the phone number, the court's. Before I could answer it, I could see a half-dozen additional deputies walk into our courtroom, telling me a verdict had been reached. Consistent with protocol, the judge's secretary asked that we return to the courtroom without letting me know whether a verdict had been reached. Over the years, I had learned to guess the reason for returning to the courtroom by paying attention to the tone of the secretary's voice on the phone. If the secretary knew you well, she might give you a verbal wink of the eye, or just come right out and tell you. In this case, the swarm of deputies inside the courtroom told me all I needed to know. When a verdict is to be read, additional deputies come inside the courtroom to be prepared for any adverse reaction by the defendant or people in the gallery. Any time a defendant faces time in jail away from his or her family and friends, emotions can boil to the surface when a jury announces a guilty verdict. Emotions can also boil to the surface when an innocent verdict is announced, especially when a victim's family and friends are in the courtroom. The worst-case scenario is when the courtroom is divided among supporters for the defendant and supporters for the victim. I have seen fights break out in the gallery after a particular verdict.

John did not need me to tell him a verdict had been reached to know what was happening. He was immediately on his phone, telling Sara to come back to the courtroom. As we waited for Sara, we did not speak. By now, I had explained every possible outcome to John and given every possible word of encouragement. There was nothing I could say at that moment that would make the next few minutes of John's life any easier. Nor would it make my life any easier.

The moments before a verdict is announced are the longest and most agonizing moments a criminal defense attorney will face. While petty compared to the feelings experienced by the client, those moments are the culmination of hours and hours of work, late nights spent at the office reviewing police reports and transcripts, hours of telephone calls and conferences with the client and his or her family, and sleepless nights spent grappling over possible defense strategies. Criminal cases that proceed to trial can last for years and, often, an attorney cannot help developing a personal relationship with the client and the client's family, who have chosen to place their lives in your hands. All of those dynamics come into play in the moments before a verdict is announced.

The court's head deputy motioned for us to come inside the courtroom. When we entered, the prosecutor was already seated at his table, head slung low, not acknowledging our presence. John and I sat at the defense table, while Sara took her customary seat in the front row of the gallery. In front of the judge's bench sat the judge's secretary and clerk and the stenographer that recorded everything that was said during the trial. Five deputies stood at strategic points around the outside of the room. Eventually, the judge walked into the room, and one of the deputies announced, "All rise." Everyone stood up and sat back down after the judge took the bench.

The judge wasted no time in announcing what we already knew, that the jury had reached a verdict. After confirming that no one had any issues to discuss, the judge requested that the jury be escorted into the courtroom. As they entered the courtroom single file, I dared not look at the jurors. Often you can figure out the verdict just by observing the faces and demeanor of the jurors as they enter the courtroom. If they are smiling or seem relaxed, it usually means the verdict is not guilty. If the jurors refuse to look at you and your client, it usually means a guilty verdict is coming. I never look at them.

The jurors took their seats, and the judge noted for the record that all jurors were present. The judge then directed the jury's foreman (usually the first juror selected during jury selection) to confirm that a verdict had been reached. To the extent there was any sound at all in the courtroom before that moment, it ceased. The foreman stated that a verdict had been reached, and the judge asked, "On the count of manslaughter in the first degree, how do you find the defendant, guilty or not guilty?" Without hesitation, the foreman looked John straight in the eye and announced…

Introduction

The meeting I had with John and Sara occurs in just about every case. Of course, sometimes the meeting occurs in a jail, and not every client has a wife or family that attends. And in every case, at some point in time, earlier or later, the time will come when my client wants to know whether he or she should plead guilty or take the case to trial.

I will not tell a client what he or she should do. What a client should do is a personal decision that only the client can make. My job is to give the client every piece of relevant information I can to make that client's decision as informed as possible. Depending on when that time comes, I may be in possession of little more than my notes recording what the client told me and, maybe, tickets and/or reports prepared by the arresting officers. Although it is ideal, for both myself and the client, to wait as long as possible before deciding whether to proceed to trial or plead guilty, sometimes that is simply not possible. Sometimes the prosecutor demands an answer to a plea offer before I have even had the opportunity, or legal right, to obtain all of the relevant evidence. In those cases, I can only speculate what might happen in the case based upon what evidence might exist.

The purpose of this book is to provide a comprehensive guide to understanding the criminal trial process and to provide you, as the reader, with the knowledge and tools needed to make the right decision, should you ever find yourself in a situation like John found himself in as he sat in my office years ago. I recognize that every criminal case is unique, just like every client is unique, and no book can provide a magic formula for making the right decision every time. Nor should anyone use this book as a substitute for hiring an attorney. That said, I am confident that every person charged with a crime or close with a person charged with a crime can find value on these pages.

1

The Reasons for Taking a Case to Trial

Trial: *n.* A formal inquiry designed to prove and put upon record the blameless characters of judges, advocates, and jurors.

"There can be an almost infinite number of reasons why a client might decide to proceed to trial—mere principle, the client doesn't care if he goes to jail (three hots and a cot at no cost can have some appeal), the client likes the attention, etc."—Ambrose Bierce, American writer

I Am Not Guilty

In New York, as in most states, absent one rarely used exception, a judge cannot accept a defendant's plea of guilty unless the judge believes the defendant has sufficiently admitted guilt. Thus, if you wish to plead guilty, you must actually admit guilt to every element of the charge to which the defendant is pleading. For example, if you decided to plead guilty to petit larceny, you would be required to admit, on the record, that you took possession of whatever it is you are accused of stealing, that you did not have permission to take possession of the item, and that you knew you did not have permission to take it. If you deny any element of the offense, the judge cannot accept your plea of guilty.

Some judges are stricter about this rule than others. Onc judge in a petit larceny case may only require the defendant to admit that, on the date in question, he intentionally took something from the grocery store without paying for it and without the permission of the store. Another judge might require the defendant to tell the court that he took two candy bars and concealed the bars in his coat pocket before leaving the store. But regardless of the degree of detail required by the judge, there usually must be some admission of guilt. If you intend to plead guilty to a crime, you must be aware of this beforehand. Otherwise, you could find yourself in an awkward situation when the judge asks you to tell him, in front of a packed courtroom, how, and sometimes even why, you chose to steal a $1.00 candy bar.

This can be harder than it might appear, especially when you might have your own doubts regarding your guilt. Not every case is as clear-cut as stealing a candy bar from a grocery store. In the case I mentioned in the Foreword, my client John did not deny punching the man in the bar, but he felt he needed to do it to defend himself and his friend. John very well might have chosen to plead guilty and not go to trial. But if he had done so, he would have done so without completely believing in his own guilt.

I have had a number of cases where, despite my clear explanation to my clients that they would need to admit every element of the crime to which they were pleading guilty, when the time came, they could not bring themselves to do it. Sometimes it might just be one element of the crime that causes a moment of self-doubt. Pleading guilty to driving while intoxicated (DWI) can sometimes lead to problems for a defendant because often the defendant admits he or she drank alcohol before operating a motor vehicle, but truly believes he or she drank less than the arresting office wrote in his report. I have had judges reject the plea because the judge believed the defendant was not being completely honest or, in the opinion of the judge, the amount of alcohol the defendant claims he or she drank could not have caused the defendant's blood alcohol content (BAC) to exceed the legal limit.

An even bigger problem is when you are innocent. The reality is, despite the rules to the contrary, defendants plead guilty or "cop out" for all kinds of reasons other than being guilty. Our criminal justice system is far from perfect. Innocent people are convicted all of the time. And defendants generally face more time in jail following a verdict at trial than they would have had they just pled guilty. So for many defendants, it is just safer to plead guilty and hedge their bet. Despite the laws that are in place to prevent people from being arrested and subsequently convicted without a certain level of evidence, there are times when innocent people are arrested and face a mountain of evidence against them.

There really is such a thing as being in the wrong place at the wrong time. Take, for example, a client I had who was charged with first-degree robbery for allegedly committing an armed robbery against two teenagers. The teenagers had their cell phones taken from them. They told the police that a black man wearing a red shirt and black pants took their phones while they were walking home late one night. About thirty minutes after the boys were robbed, my client was spotted by police walking home from work near the scene of the crime wearing a red shirt and black pants. The police stopped my client and later seized from him one of the phones taken from one of the boys. My client was immediately arrested and, if convicted, faced a long time in prison as a result of a previous felony conviction.

After being retained and meeting my client, I learned that my client had, in fact, just gotten out of work near the scene of the crime before being arrested and, before leaving work, had purchased the subject phone from a friend who had stopped by his place of employment, offering the phone for sale. While it may sound like a convenient excuse created to avoid getting in trouble, I believed him. His story checked out by our investigators, and I genuinely believed in his innocence. But my faith in his innocence did not insulate him from the strong evidence of his guilt—the matching description, his presence near the scene of the crime, and his possession of one of the phones.

The prosecutor in the case made a plea offer that would have guaranteed that he serve just a fraction of what he was likely to get if he proceeded to trial and lost. It essentially would have guaranteed that he would not spend the prime of his life behind bars. Here was a case where, although I believed my client was innocent, and my client stated he was innocent, it made perfect sense for him to take the plea deal and plead guilty. But to do so, assuming he really was innocent, would have required him to, in essence, commit perjury—to lie to the court so he could accept the plea offer. It was a true conundrum. Fortunately, my client decided to reject the offer, and he went on to be acquitted following a jury trial. But this situation does occur, and when it does, it puts both the defendant and the attorney in an awkward position.

I mentioned that there are some rarely used exceptions. One exception is pleading guilty pursuant to what is commonly referred to as an Alford or, in West Virginia, a Kennedy plea, or pleading *nolo contendere*, which translates into "I do not wish to contend" or, simply, no contest. Whether you can plead no contest depends on the particular state in which you are being prosecuted, as every state has its own rules governing pleading. If you are allowed to plead no contest, you need only state that you do not wish to contest the allegations made against you. You do not need to admit any specific allegations. Similarly, under an Alford or Kennedy plea, you would only be required to admit that sufficient evidence exists with which the prosecution is likely able to prove its case beyond a reasonable doubt. Again, you would not have to admit guilt or any specific allegation.

In many states, such as New York, to plead guilty without admitting guilt, you must first obtain the consent of the prosecutor and the approval of the judge. Such pleas are very uncommon and are generally reserved for sex cases, where admitting guilt can mandate that you register as a sex offender. Thus, if you intend to plead guilty, you must be prepared to admit enough facts to support every element of the particular crime. If you honestly do not believe you are guilty, or simply cannot bring yourself to admit guilt before the court, you will likely be forced to take your case to trial.

In addition to admitting guilt, you must also demonstrate to the court that you are doing so knowingly, voluntarily, and intelligently. Before a court can accept a plea of guilty, it must conduct what is commonly referred to as a plea colloquy. The US Supreme Court, our country's highest court, mandates that a court, before it can accept a plea of guilty, must ensure the plea is made intelligently, knowingly, and voluntarily. Towards that end, the court must advise you of the nature of the charge, the potential penalties that might result from the plea of guilty, including the applicable sentencing range, and your right to not plead guilty and request a jury trial. The judge must ask you if you understand each of these points, and you must give an affirmative response on the record.

Many judges use a script to ensure that all of the questions are asked. And after receiving an affirmative response, the court will state on the record that, in sum and substance, based on your oral responses and physical mannerisms, the judge believes you have made an intelligent, knowing, and voluntary plea. The purpose of this is to ensure you are pleading guilty not only because you are guilty, but because you want to plead guilty. This is why the judge will usually also ask you if you are under the influence of drugs or alcohol, if you have had sufficient time to discuss your decision with your attorney, and whether any promises have been made by any person, other than any sentencing promise by the court, to get you to plead guilty. A failure by the court to do this could provide you with grounds to attack the plea at a later date, including a motion for leave to vacate the plea of guilty. However, as I always tell my clients, if you are already thinking about how you can take back your plea, you probably should not be pleading guilty in the first place.

You have the right to be instructed on these issues by your attorney, and you should always meet with your attorney in advance of court to make sure you are fully prepared to say all of things the court and prosecutor will require before they will accept your plea of guilty. That said, no matter how much time you spend preparing, there always remains the real possibility that nerves or some other distraction might cause you to forget something in court. This is why you are also entitled to have your attorney present with you when you plead guilty.

There Is No Plea Offer

In the majority of criminal cases, the prosecutor will make a plea offer. In a felony case, this could occur before or after the case is presented to the grand jury. Prosecutors have their own reasons for wanting to settle cases short of trial. For starters, it would be physically impossible to try every case. There are only so many prosecutors, and it is not uncommon for one prosecutor to handle a hundred or more cases. This is especially true in state cases, as the prosecutors who prosecute state cases do not have as much input into what cases they choose to prosecute as federal prosecutors do.

Money is also an issue for prosecutors. Offices such as the district attorney's office in New York have limited budgets. Criminal cases can become expensive, particularly when expert witnesses must be retained and paid. Major felonies such as homicide cases often require the services of multiple experts, experts the district attorney's office does not employ. Thus, prosecutors must be fiscally responsible in choosing which cases to take a hard stance on. This is why it often makes sense for a defendant in New York charged with aggravated unlicensed operation to take the case to trial. To prove this charge, the people must prove, beyond a reasonable doubt, that the defendant knew his or her license was suspended. The people cannot prove a defendant knew his or her license was suspended without putting someone employed by the New York State Department of Motor Vehicles in Albany on the stand to testify. The cost to do this is generally too great a burden on a district attorney's office and, as a result, it will usually not be prepared to move forward on the day of trial, resulting in a dismissal of the charge.

There is, however, no guarantee that a plea offer will be made in your case. In DWI cases, for example, many prosecutorial offices have strict policies on when they will make an offer. In Monroe County in New York, the district attorney's office will usually not offer a reduction of a DWI where the defendant's BAC is above 0.12 percent. In other cases, there may not be an offer because the case has caught the attention of the media, and the district attorney prosecuting the case is up for reelection soon. This is why it is critical that your attorney be tuned in to all of the dynamics of your case, including the probability that a better offer, or any offer, will be forthcoming. Sometimes this means knowing whether you should reject an offer because it is likely a better one will be made on the eve of trial. Or rejecting an offer because it is likely the same offer will be available on the eve of trial after you have exhausted all of your opportunities to have the case dismissed. There is nothing worse than turning down an offer early in a case and proceeding to trial half-heartedly, only to find that another offer is not going to be made.

If an offer is not made, you have no choice in the matter. You must either go to trial or plead guilty to the charges. There are times when, even though there is no offer, you should still consider foregoing trial and pleading guilty to the charges. The most obvious case is where, if you are convicted, you face a determinate sentence. A determinate sentence is when the judge must sentence you to serve a fixed time in jail between a minimum and maximum range. For example, let us say you are charged with a crime where, if convicted, you must serve a determinate sentence of anywhere between five and fifteen years. In this case, the judge could sentence you to serve anywhere from five years in jail up to fifteen years in jail.

Any time you face a determinate sentence if convicted, you must take into consideration the likelihood that the sentencing judge will likely give you some consideration for pleading guilty and saving both the court and the prosecution the time and expense of going through a trial. In other words, judges generally like to provide defendants with some incentive to plead guilty, even when there is no plea offer made by the prosecutor. Knowing a particular judge's propensity for sentencing will help you make the decision of whether to plead guilty. If your attorney is not familiar with the judge in your case, he or she must confide with others that do before he gives you meaningful advice.

The Benefit Outweighs the Risk

I have discussed two primary reasons to take a case to trial. The third reason is probably the most likely reason a person would decide to take a case to trial: the potential benefit of going to trial outweighs the potential risks. It is a formula most of us use in our everyday lives to make decisions, sometimes without even realizing it. Any time someone has a choice to make between two compelling options, there is a certain amount of risk/benefit analysis occurring. Do I stay for one more drink or go home to my family? Do I take a new job offer or stay with my current employer? The choices can be menial, like whether to stay for that extra drink, or potentially life-changing, like deciding whether to take that job offer or proceed to trial.

The potential major benefit and risk of going to trial is obvious: winning and losing. The more challenging aspect of the analysis is determining the probabilities of winning and losing. To be convicted, the prosecutor bears the sole burden of proving every element of the charges beyond a reasonable doubt. Thus, if you are charged with petit larceny, the prosecutor must prove, beyond a reasonable doubt, that you took possession of another's property, that you did so knowingly, and that you did so without permission.

The definition of reasonable doubt may differ slightly from one jurisdiction to another. The following is the typical definition read to juries in New York before they begin their deliberations:

> The law uses the term "proof beyond a reasonable doubt" to tell you how convincing the evidence of guilt must be to permit a verdict of guilty. The law recognizes that, in dealing with human affairs, there are very few things in this world that we know with absolute certainty. Therefore, the law does not require the people to prove a defendant guilty beyond all possible doubt. On the other hand, it is not sufficient to prove that the defendant is probably guilty. In a criminal case, the proof of guilt must be stronger than that. It must be beyond a reasonable doubt.
>
> A reasonable doubt is an honest doubt of the defendant's guilt for which a reason exists based upon the nature and quality of the evidence. It is an actual doubt, not an imaginary doubt. It is a doubt that a reasonable person, acting in a matter of this importance, would be likely to entertain because of the evidence that was presented or because of the lack of convincing evidence.
>
> Proof of guilt beyond a reasonable doubt is proof that leaves you so firmly convinced of the defendant's guilt that you have no reasonable doubt of the existence of any element of the crime or of the defendant's identity as the person who committed the crime.
>
> In determining whether the people have proven the defendant's guilt beyond a reasonable doubt, you should

> be guided solely by a full and fair evaluation of the evidence. After carefully evaluating the evidence, each of you must decide whether that evidence convinces you beyond a reasonable doubt of the defendant's guilt.
>
> Whatever your verdict may be, it must not rest upon baseless speculations.
>
> Nor may it be influenced in any way by bias, prejudice, sympathy, or by a desire to bring an end to your deliberations or avoid an unpleasant duty.
>
> If you are not convinced beyond a reasonable doubt that the defendant is guilty of a charged crime, you must find the defendant not guilty of that crime. If you are convinced beyond a reasonable doubt that the defendant is guilty of a charged crime, you must find the defendant guilty of that crime.

Whether reasonable doubt has been proven is decided by either a judge in a bench trial or a jury in a jury trial. The difference between the two trials is discussed in more detail later in the book.

Most often, by the time you are faced with having to make the decision of whether to proceed to trial, you and your attorney have a decent grasp of the strengths and weaknesses of the prosecution's case against you and the strength of any defenses you may have. Where a bench trial is decided upon, your attorney should also have some level of knowledge regarding the particular judge's propensity for deciding cases similar to yours. For example, if you are taking a DWI case to trial with a known BAC, your attorney should know the history of the judge (i.e., how often that judge will reduce the DWI to a lesser offense such as DWAI, or drinking while ability impaired). Some judges are known for almost always reducing the charge following a trial, even when the prosecutor has proven that your BAC was above the legal limit. The opposite is true of other judges. There can exist significant disparity between the ruling tendencies of even judges in the same court. While one judge in Greece

Town Court might almost always reduce a DWI when a defendant's BAC is 0.14 or lower, another judge in the same court may rarely ever reduce the charge with the same BAC. For more information on the importance of having an attorney with knowledge of the judge presiding over a DWI case, see Aspatore's 2012 book entitled, *Strategies for Defending DWI Cases in New York.*

The decision of whether to take your case to trial is more difficult when the decision must be made before you have all of the proof in the case. As stated above, this is usually not the case. In felony cases, most state's rules of evidence do not require that the prosecutor disclose all of the proof in the case until after you have been indicted, and the case has been transferred from a local court to a superior court. Thus, any time you are faced with a plea offer before being indicted, your decision of whether to accept the offer may need to be made before having possession of all of the evidence in the case. Now, simply rejecting a pre-indictment plea offer does not equate to deciding on a trial, but any offer made before indictment will usually not be available once you are indicted. Thus, by rejecting a pre-indictment offer, you are often sealing your fate, making trial a high probability.

Most attorneys shy away from quantifying a client's chances of winning and losing at trial. They fear that, if they tell their clients they have a 75 percent chance of winning, and the client is convicted, a grievance may be filed against them or, at worst, a malpractice lawsuit commenced. Ethical rules prohibit an attorney from guaranteeing a result. But they do not prohibit an attorney from giving an honest opinion based upon the information at their disposal. I believe an attorney is doing his or her client a great disservice by not making some estimation. Without an estimation, a client cannot make an informed decision. That is why I almost always estimate my client's chances of winning and losing. Of course, I inform my clients that it is only my opinion and remind them that I cannot predict what will actually happen with certainty. There are simply too many variables and factors, many unforeseeable, to accurately predict a result. For example, you can never be sure of the composition of the jury pool from which you must select your jury. An unknown witness may suddenly come to light, or the judge may make an adverse ruling on a piece of evidence you did not expect. Nevertheless, I believe an attorney should do his or her best to draw upon his or her experience, knowledge of the court, judge, and prosecutor, and overall expertise to guestimate the odds of winning or losing.

This also requires that you determine what constitutes a win and a loss for you. It would be a tremendous oversimplification to think only in terms of winning and losing, without understanding what exactly constitutes a win and a loss for you. Winning and losing is not white and black.

Take the DWI case, for example. In New York, for instance, DWI is a class misdemeanor. If convicted, you would have a crime added to your rap sheet, and you could be sentenced up to one year in local jail. As stated earlier, following bench trials, judges frequently find defendants not guilty of the DWI charges and, instead, find the defendant guilty of the lesser charge of DWAI, which is a violation, not a crime. Thus, if you were convicted of DWAI, there would be no added blemish to your rap sheet, and you can legally be sentenced to serve no more than fifteen days in local jail. For those reasons, the majority of defendants would consider being convicted of DWAI a win.

That is not the case, however, for everyone. Take, for example, the person who cannot afford to endure any suspension of his or her driver's license. When you are convicted of DWAI in New York, you still face a three-month suspension of your driver's license. Or, for someone who cannot afford to serve time in jail, a conviction with a sentence with just probation might be considered a victory. For another, winning might mean being convicted of only a misdemeanor and not a felony. The point is that what is good for the goose is not necessarily good for the gander. And what constitutes a win for one person may not necessarily constitute a win for another. Therefore, you must decide what results you consider a win before you can even attempt to assess the probabilities of that result occurring. And once you decide what outcomes are acceptable and which ones are not, you can then estimate the chances of all of the potential outcomes, including those that are acceptable, and choose whether to proceed to trial.

Once you have a general idea of what the probabilities are of winning and losing, the final step is to decide whether your odds of winning justify taking the risk of losing. It is a question every sports better must ask before placing a bet. Say, for example, you were contemplating betting ten dollars on your favorite football team winning, and you estimate that your team will win the game 51 percent of the time. Does the benefit of winning the game outweigh the risk of losing? Clearly, in this example, winning means ten extra dollars in your pocket, and losing means ten fewer dollars in your pocket. Knowing it is more likely you will win than lose, you must decide how important the benefit of winning ten dollars is compared to the risk of losing the same amount. If you were independently wealthy, losing ten dollars may be of little consequence. To the contrary, if that ten dollars is the difference between being able or unable to pay the mortgage this month on your house, the risk of losing may simply be too great, no matter how good your odds are of winning that bet.

This is the basic premise behind risk/benefit analysis. You must decide, now knowing what constitutes a win and a loss, whether the benefits of winning at trial outweigh the risks of losing. Unfortunately, there is no fool-proof mathematical formula, no $pi = mc^2$ to apply to your case. It is part science and part art. And I cannot stress more the importance of having an experienced and talented attorney to help you make the decision. But if you apply these basic principles, you will increase your chances of making the right decision.

2

Trial Preparation

"Trials are won or lost before they even begin." —Anonymous

Trial is the conclusion of any criminal case, notwithstanding a possible appeal if convicted. But trial cannot be looked at in a vacuum. The success or failure of trial is the culmination of many decisions that are made the moment you are charged with a crime. The majority of this book focuses on the trial itself, but it would be irresponsible not to talk through some of the mileposts that line the road leading to trial.

Representation

One of the most fundamental features of our criminal justice system is a defendant's right to the assistance of counsel. In New York, attorneys are required to post inside their office what is called a "Client Statement of Rights," sometimes referred to as a "Bill of Rights." They are as follows:

1. You are entitled to be treated with courtesy and consideration at all times by your lawyer and the other lawyers and non-lawyer personnel in your lawyer's office.
2. You are entitled to have your attorney handle your legal matter competently and diligently, in accordance with the highest standards of the profession. If you are not satisfied with how your matter is being handled, you have the right to discharge your attorney and terminate the attorney-client relationship at any time. (Court approval may be required in some matters, and your attorney may have a claim against you for the value of services rendered to you up to the point of discharge.)

3. You are entitled to your lawyer's independent professional judgment and undivided loyalty uncompromised by conflicts of interest.
4. You are entitled to be charged reasonable fees and expenses and to have your lawyer explain before or within a reasonable time after commencement of the representation how the fees and expenses will be computed and the manner and frequency of billing. You are entitled to request and receive a written itemized bill from your attorney at reasonable intervals. You may refuse to enter into any arrangement for fees and expenses you find unsatisfactory. In the event of a fee dispute, you may have the right to seek arbitration; your attorney will provide you with the necessary information regarding arbitration in the event of a fee dispute, or upon your request.
5. You are entitled to have your questions and concerns addressed promptly and to receive a prompt reply to your letters, telephone calls, emails, faxes, and other communications.
6. You are entitled to be kept reasonably informed as to the status of your matter and are entitled to have your attorney promptly comply with your reasonable requests for information, including your requests for copies of papers relevant to the matter. You are entitled to sufficient information to allow you to participate meaningfully in the development of your matter and make informed decisions regarding the representation.
7. You are entitled to have your legitimate objectives respected by your attorney. In particular, the decision of whether to settle your matter is yours and not your lawyer's. (Court approval of a settlement is required in some matters.)
8. You have the right to privacy in your communications with your lawyer and to have your confidential information preserved by your lawyer to the extent required by law.
9. You are entitled to have your attorney conduct himself or herself ethically in accordance with the New York Rules of Professional Conduct.
10. You may not be refused representation on the basis of race, creed, color, religion, sex, sexual orientation, age, national origin, or disability.

These are your basic rights after you have retained an attorney. But you also have the right to counsel, which means you have the right to retain an attorney of your choosing to represent you during the criminal case and, if you cannot afford to hire an attorney, to have one appointed to represent you by the court. If you cannot afford an attorney, the court will usually appoint a public defender to represent you. A public defender is an attorney who is employed by the county or state, whose sole responsibility is to represent defendants who do not have the financial resources to hire their own attorney.

To determine if you qualify for a public defender, you must provide information proving your income, usually tax returns or recent pay stubs. The income limit to qualify for a public defender is usually very low. Eligibility for a public defender varies from state to state. Some states require that your income not exceed a certain amount to qualify. Other states, like New York, base eligibility on the defendant's ability to afford an attorney, not an inflexible income threshold. New York courts have discretion in determining whether a defendant can afford to hire counsel, and can consider numerous factors, including the defendant's current financial obligations, including child support obligations.

If you do qualify for a public defender, you could still be appointed a private attorney to represent you. In this case, the private attorney would be paid by the government, like a public defender would. Often, a conflict of interest prohibits the public defender from representing you, requiring the appointment of a private attorney. Conflicts of interest arise frequently in cases where there are multiple co-defendants or where the public defender's office has represented the victim in your case in the past. For example, had my client John and two other friends at the bar been accused of assault, the public defender's office would be prohibited from representing more than one of the defendants, as there would exist an obvious potential conflict of interest. Say, for instance, part of John's defense included accusing one of the other co-defendants of being the person who struck the victim over the head with the beer bottle. The public defender would then be representing two clients with conflicting interests. In such a case, the public defender's office would be appointed by the court to represent one of the co-defendants, and the court would appoint private counsel to represent the other co-defendant, unless the other co-defendants retained their own private counsel.

If you do qualify for the services of a public defender, you are not prohibited from still hiring a private attorney of your choosing, assuming you have the financial resources. If you qualify for a public defender, and there is no conflict necessitating the appointment of private counsel, you will be faced with the choice of either being represented by a public defender or hiring a private attorney.

One of the most common questions I am asked by prospective clients is: should I hire a private attorney? Most people automatically assume the choice is an easy one; you hire a private attorney. There is a great stigma associated with public defenders or, as they are often referred to on the streets, public pretenders. Public defenders have a bad, and I believe unwarranted, reputation as being incompetent. People automatically assume that because they are not paid a lot of money, they are somehow less able than their counterpart private attorneys.

While there are certainly incompetent public defenders, I do not believe, proportionately, there are any more incompetent public defenders than there are incompetent private attorneys. This is especially true when comparing public defenders to private attorneys representing defendants in felony cases. Typically, the more senior and experienced public defenders are the ones charged with representing defendants in felony cases. It is the less serious cases, such as cases involving only misdemeanor charges, where it is more likely you will be represented by a younger and less experienced public defender.

In fact, public defenders are often more experienced than most private attorneys. Statistically, the average public defender handles more trials in a calendar year than the average private attorney. Most graduate from the same colleges and law schools that private attorneys graduate from, and they pass the same bar examination.

Okay, so now that I have that off my chest, you are probably expecting that I recommend that you, assuming you qualify for their services, accept representation by a public defender. But you would be wrong. I recommend that, if you can afford a private attorney, you do so. Just not for the reasons you probably think. The primary reason I recommend hiring a private attorney is the workload of the typical public defender. The sad reality is that most, if not all, public defender offices are horribly underfunded and understaffed. There are too many defendants to represent and too few public defenders to represent them. As of 2009, the National Legal Aid and Defender Association recommended that a public defender handle no more than 150 cases at one time. Many public defenders handle twice that amount at any given time. Studies have shown that, with those caseloads, public defenders simply do not have enough time to provide adequate and competent representation. If you are represented by a public defender, it is unlikely you will receive a lot of one-on-one attention. Do not expect timely return calls or regular visits at the jail if you are in custody. Do not expect that you will receive timely responses to correspondence, and do not expect your attorney will set aside much time for you during court appearances, as it is likely your attorney will have numerous clients to attend to.

When you are appointed a public defender, you also do not get to choose which public defender represents you. The court appoints the public defender's office, and someone in the office chooses which public defender will handle your case. You might get the office's best attorney, or you might get the office's worst attorney. Further, it is very unlikely that you will have the same attorney on a consistent basis throughout the case. Public defenders often have other attorneys in their office cover court appearances because of obligations in other courts. This means you often will not know who will be with you in court from one appearance to the next.

Beyond just the issue of competency, there is the issue of rapport. The client/attorney relationship is a lot like a marriage. In fact, it often lasts longer than the average marriage, as cases can drag on for years. And like marriages, sometimes they just do not work. You need to have confidence in your attorney. You need to trust your attorney. When you have the ability to hire a private attorney, you can speak with numerous attorneys and select the one you believe is best suited to represent you. One that is compatible with you and imbues in you confidence. It is your choice and not the choice of the court or the head of the public defender's office. And you can choose an attorney who can commit to personally being present with you in court and not sending an associate without your knowledge.

So, how do you know if you can afford a private attorney? You cannot afford a private attorney simply because you have the money to pay the attorney's fee. If you choose to hire a private attorney, it is critical that you not only have the resources to pay the attorney's fee, but any necessary expenses. Most criminal attorneys charge either a flat fee or charge by the hour at an agreed upon hourly rate. Under a flat fee arrangement, the attorney will charge one or multiple lump sums for his or her services. For example, the attorney may charge $5,000 for all required services in the case, including trial, or he or she may break it up—say $2,500 for all services performed before trial and, if the case proceeds to trial, an additional $2,500 for trial. The attorney may require the whole amount up front or may accept partial payments pursuant to a payment plan.

Under an hourly fee arrangement, the attorney will agree to charge you a certain amount for every hour expended on your case, such as $150 per hour. The attorney may require an up-front retainer or deposit with him or her to bill against as time is accrued, or may simply bill you at the end of each month, with nothing due up front.

Under either arrangement, out-of-pocket expenses are almost always additional. Out-of-pocket expenses can include postage, document copying, process servers, experts, private investigators, jury consultants, and court transcripts. Some expenses, such as copying and postage, are unavoidable. Others are optional but often critical to carrying out an effective defense, such as the expense associated with hiring a private investigator and expert. Private investigators usually charge by the hour, and depending on how much private investigation is needed, it can easily cost between $500 and $10,000 at the end of the day. Experts, such as medical experts, ballistics experts, and forensic experts, also usually charge by the hour, and can run between $1,000 and $25,000. If you are represented by a public defender, these expenses are covered. If not, you must foot the bill, and depending on the limit to your financial resources, you may or may not be able to afford to hire everyone recommended by your attorney. Thus, before you choose to hire a private attorney instead of accepting representation by a public defender, you should ask prospective private attorneys what expenses they anticipate, including which ones they believe are absolutely necessary. Do not hire a private attorney before you know you can really afford to do so.

The following is a basic flat fee retainer agreement:

> MCKAIN LAW FIRM, P.C.
> 1 EAST MAIN STREET, SUITE 711
> ROCHESTER, NEW YORK 14614
>
> RETAINER AGREEMENT
>
> Simon Says does hereby engage and employ the McKain Law Firm, P.C. (the "Firm"), to represent me in connection with a certain criminal matter, to wit: Possession of Stolen Property and related charges pending in Canandaigua City Court. Said representation shall include all aspects of the criminal case, including any trial. Said representation shall not include representation relating to any forfeiture proceedings, violation of probation/parole matters, or post-conviction matters, including appeals. In the event services are required for any of the above-omitted matters; or the client faces charges beyond the Firm's knowledge at the time this agreement is executed, including without limitation, additional unknown charges or felony charges; or the client makes any material misrepresentations of fact, the Firm shall be entitled to cancel this agreement.
>
> For such professional services in connection with the criminal matter, I hereby agree to pay the amount of $1,500.00 for all services performed, which fee shall be due at the commencement of representation.
>
> I understand that I am also obligated to pay for any expenses and disbursements that may be incurred, including without

limitation, expert fees, filing fees, process service fees, and testimony and investigative fees. Should said fees be necessary, the Firm shall obtain your express authorization prior to incurring any such expenses on your behalf.

In the event you terminate this agreement prior to completion of all services, you are entitled to a return of any unused fees. In such case, the Firm shall be entitled to be paid on an hourly basis using the following rates:

Kevin K. McKain, Esq.:	$200.00 per hour
Associates:	$150.00 per hour

You understand that the Firm cannot make any promises to you concerning the outcome of this case, other than to inform you that we will render our best professional skill.

I ACKNOWLEDGE BEFORE SIGNING THIS CONTRACT THAT I HAVE RECEIVED AND READ IT AND UNDERSTAND THE STATEMENTS MADE HEREIN AND HAVE RECEIVED A COPY OF IT.

Dated: February 18, 2015

____

SIMON SAYS

ACCEPTED:

____

Kevin K. McKain, Esq.

Private Investigators, Experts, and Consultants

Private investigators, experts, and consultants are people you hire to help your attorney prepare for trial and during trial. Not every case warrants the hiring of a private investigator, expert, or consultant. It is your attorney's duty to consider their possible benefit and make the appropriate recommendation to you.

Of all possible outside help hired in the typical criminal defense case, private investigators are the most common and probably the most important. They are frequently used by both the prosecution and the defense. Private investigators are people trained to do exactly what their name implies: investigate. But investigation is only one aspect of their usefulness in contributing to your defense. While the particular case dictates the exact scope of their investigation, private investigators can identify, locate, interview, and take statements from potential witnesses; visit and photograph the crime scene and any physical evidence; investigate the background, including criminal history, of anticipated trial witnesses; vet expert witnesses; obtain surveillance videos; surveil witnesses; analyze discovery; serve subpoenas and other documents; and otherwise act as a second set of eyes and ears for your attorney.

I believe a private investigator should be retained in almost every felony criminal case (not to imply that one should not at least be seriously considered when charged with a misdemeanor). At a minimum, a private investigator should visit the crime scene, visit the location of your arrest and any other important locations, as well as interview every potential witness. Interviewing witnesses through a private investigator is important because neither you nor your attorney can do it without risking a dilemma at trial.

By taking statements from a witness, the private investigator becomes a witness him or herself, one who could potentially be called at trial to testify. Say, for example, a witness at the bar my client John was at tells my private investigator that, before John swung the bottle, the man he struck had pulled a knife on him. At trial, the man is called as a witness by the prosecutor and, when asked what happened that night, he testifies that John was unprovoked when he struck the man with a beer bottle. On cross-examination, I ask the witness whether the man had pulled out a knife, and he testifies that he saw no knife. When I next ask him whether he recalls telling my private investigator that he saw a knife, he denies that too. Luckily for John, I had my private investigator standing by to testify. I put the investigator on the stand, and he testifies that he interviewed the witness, and the witness told him he saw a knife. Even better, had the investigator gotten a written statement from the witness, the written statement could have been used to show that the witness is being dishonest. Now, if your attorney had conducted the interview, you would be out of luck, as your attorney cannot testify on your behalf and represent you at the same time.

Unlike private investigators, experts are people hired for their expertise on specific issues in your case. Possible experts are endless. It is your attorney's responsibility to identify the specific needs of your case. While not exhaustive, the following are a few common experts utilized in criminal cases:

1. *DNA expert.* DNA evidence has become increasingly more common and sophisticated in criminal investigations and cases. For example, one expert testifying for the prosecution might give the opinion that his or her analysis of DNA in a sexual assault case revealed that the suspect was not excluded as a potential contributor to a recovered semen sample. Another expert called by the defendant could give the opinion that the very same test result proved that 10 percent of the male population may similarly not be excluded. Had you not hired your own expert, the jury would have only seen one side of the coin.
2. *Ballistic expert.* Ballistics deals with the mechanics of projectiles. In the criminal context, it usually refers to firearms. Ballistics experts can give opinions on the type of firearm and ammunition used in the alleged crime, the distance between the shooter and victim, and whether a particular bullet was fired from a particular firearm, to name a few.
3. *Medical expert.* Medical experts can include everything from a medical examiner who can give an opinion on how a person died to a psychologist or psychiatrist who can give the opinion that a wife accused of killing her husband suffered from extreme emotional distress.
4. *Jury consultant.* A jury consultant is a person who specializes in predicting how a prospective juror will respond to the evidence

that is expected to be presented at trial. For a defendant, a jury consultant's job is to help the defendant's attorney pick the best jurors (i.e., jurors who are most likely to find the defendant not guilty). Jury consultants are uncommon, except on high-profile cases and the most serious of felony offenses. And like any expert, they are very expensive.

3

The Types of Trials

"The criminal trial today is...a kind of show-jumping contest in which the rider for the prosecution must clear every obstacle to succeed."
—Robert Mark, British police commissioner

Trial is generally defined as an examination and determination of the law and facts of the case. As will be discussed in greater length later, in a jury trial, the jury determines the facts and the judge determines the law. In a bench trial, the judge determines both the law and the facts.

In most states, including New York, you have the right to a trial when charged with any offense, whether the offense is a misdemeanor, felony, or violation. Felonies and misdemeanors are criminal offenses or crimes. Violations are considered non-criminal offenses. Felonies are the most severe charge you can face, and they are generally the only classification of charges that carry with them the possibility of doing prison time, time in a state correctional facility as opposed to time in a local jail. In New York, felonies range from class A to class E, with A felonies being the most severe. If convicted of a felony, you could be sentenced to anywhere from five years probation to life in prison.

Misdemeanors are the second most severe classification of criminal offenses. In New York, misdemeanors are either classified as an A misdemeanor or a B misdemeanor. If convicted of a misdemeanor in New York, you can be sentenced to pay fines or you can be sentenced to serve as much as one year in a local jail.

Violations are non-criminal offenses. Simple traffic infractions such as speeding and illegal parking are violations. Defendants convicted of violations are rarely sentenced to serve jail time, and fines are generally the most severe sentence handed down by the judge.

At trial, you have the right to hear and challenge the evidence presented against you, usually in open court. Challenging evidence can be accomplished by cross-examining witnesses and by presenting your own evidence. In misdemeanor and felony cases, you have the right to either a jury trial or a bench trial. You do not have a right to a jury trial when charged with only a violation. In the remainder of this chapter, I will discuss the differences between bench and jury trials and trials in felony cases and misdemeanor cases.

The Bench Trial

With few exceptions, unless you are only charged with a violation, violating probation, or are entitled to mandatory youthful offender status, you may choose to have your case decided by either a bench trial or a jury trial. In most jurisdictions, the court can, under certain limited circumstances, deny a defendant the right to choose a bench trial, including situations where the court believes the defendant is only electing a bench trial to achieve an impermissible advantage. Otherwise, if you do not specifically waive a jury trial in favor of a bench trial, the court will grant you a jury trial. Most courts require the defendant to sign a written waiver of the right to a jury trial. However, this waiver can be withdrawn any time before trial, subject to the court's approval. Once a waiver is signed, it is within the court's discretion to approve or deny a request to withdraw the waiver.

In a bench trial, the judge hears the evidence, makes the decision regarding your guilt or innocence, and, if you are found guilty, sentences you. The judge is the arbiter of both the law and the facts. Bench trials are most common in misdemeanor cases, especially DWI/DUI cases where there is a chemical test result evidencing the defendant's guilt.

At risk of stating the obvious, whenever a defendant chooses to have his or her case decided by a bench trial, the defendant is electing to place his or her fate in the hands of one person. And unless I have intimate knowledge of the propensities and inclinations of the judge who would preside over a client's trial, I will almost never recommend that my client choose a bench trial. If my client is charged for the first time with DWI with a BAC of 0.12, I want to know what the judge has done on the last fifty cases where a defendant was charged for the first time with DWI with a BAC of 0.12.

Judges are, before anything else, human beings with ordinary problems, opinions, and attitudes that have been developed through experience. Judges are bound by strict ethical rules and laws from allowing their own personal views and opinions to interfere with their judicial roles. When a judge puts on the black robe, it is both literal and figurative. However, even the heaviest robe cannot prevent the human element from seeping into a judge's mind while he or she sits on the bench. Judges like to ask potential jurors during jury selection whether they can "cork the bottle." Can they put aside personal opinions, stereotypes, and biases for the sake of remaining a neutral and impartial juror? Judges face the same challenge. They, too, must try to "cork the bottle" when they preside over a bench trial.

But despite their best and most sincere attempts, even judges remain imperfect. This can be an advantage or a disadvantage. You must know enough about the judge who will preside over your trial to determine which one is the most likely. Some judges have a known proclivity for leniency on some types of charges while being unforgiving on others. Several years ago, I represented a Marine charged with possession of a handgun. My client purchased the gun while serving in Afghanistan. At the time he purchased it, he did not have a permit. He brought the gun home with him, and while he was cleaning it inside his home, the gun accidentally discharged, firing a bullet through his thigh.

In addition to being a highly decorated Marine, my client had no criminal history whatsoever, was a husband and father of two small children, and was just a salt of the earth kind of guy. The prosecutor was willing to offer my client the chance to plead guilty to a significantly reduced charge with a sentence of no jail time. However, the judge would not approve the sentence. The judge, it turned out, had a family member whom had been a victim of a shooting and absolutely detested guns. He had no sympathy for anyone accused of possessing a gun without a valid permit, military or no military, family man or no family man. I did not know this when I took the case, but it did not take long for me to catch the drift. Unwilling to accept jail time, my client elected to proceed to trial. You can probably guess what type of trial he chose. Yes, he chose to have the case heard by a jury. This was an easy decision.

Assessing how favorable the judge's disposition is towards your case is not the only consideration. There are other reasons for electing a bench trial. For example, it is generally prudent to have a judge decide your case when your defense is based on technical arguments or subtle legal distinctions. Most judges are lawyers. They graduated law school and passed the bar exam. Many actively practice law at the same time they are employed as judges. As a result, they are generally better equipped than the average non-lawyer juror to understand less obvious arguments and defenses.

I have learned this lesson the hard way. Years ago, a client of mine was charged with possessing cocaine. My client was a passenger in a vehicle occupied by three friends when the police stopped the vehicle and discovered a bag containing powder cocaine in the vehicle's glove box. My client was not driving the vehicle, and the vehicle belonged to the person who was. Aside from my client's presence inside the vehicle, there was no evidence that the cocaine belonged to my client.

When no one took responsibility for it, the police charged all four of the vehicle's occupants, including my client, with possessing the cocaine. Even though no one inside the vehicle had the drugs on him, the police charged everyone under something known as the vehicle presumption rule. Said rule, which is read to the jury before deliberations, states that when drugs are discovered inside a vehicle that is occupied by more than one person, and the drugs are not located on any one person, the jury can presume that each occupant possessed the drugs. The rule also states that the presumption can be overcome by evidence that the drugs did not belong to the defendant, and the jury has the discretion to ignore the rule.

The rule is read to the jury, along with every other law and instruction, right before the jury leaves the courtroom to begin deliberating. At least as far as a defendant is concerned, the most important part of the rule is the part that says the jury can choose to ignore any presumption. In other words, the jury is not required to presume that everyone inside the vehicle possessed the drugs.

To my complete surprise, my client was found guilty of possession. I was sure the jury could not find my client guilty based on the evidence that came out during the trial. After the jury came back with its verdict, I waited to speak with some of the jurors to find out what went wrong. Several of the jurors, on the verge of tears, explained to me that they did not believe my client possessed the cocaine but believed they had to presume he did as a result of the rule that was read to them. When I went over the rule with them and pointed out that the presumption was optional, they admitted they had misunderstood it and made a mistake.

This was not the only time I had a jury misinterpret the law and, as a consequence, find a client guilty. Part of the blame lies in the rules that govern how a jury is given the law and rules governing their deliberations. In New York, the judge reads to the jury the entire charge and does not leave the jury with the charge in writing. It can take a judge an hour or more to read it, and I believe it simply asks too much of the jury to remember everything that is read. The judge does also instruct the jury that it can request to have any part of the charge read back if it does not understand something during its deliberation, but even this does not alleviate the possibility that the jury may believe it understands something that it does not.

The point is that judges are less likely to make this kind of mistake than juries. Thus, if you have any doubts regarding a jury's ability to comprehend what is necessary to find you not guilty, you may elect a bench trial instead.

The Jury Trial

In a jury trial, a jury hears all of the evidence and facts presented at trial, applics the evidence and facts to the law, and makes the decision of whether your guilt has been proven beyond a reasonable doubt. The judge remains responsible for making rulings on any issues regarding the law. In this way, the jury becomes the judge of the facts, while the judge becomes the judge of the law.

In a jury trial, the verdict, whether guilty or not guilty, must be unanimous. Defense attorneys often joke that, while the prosecutor must convince every juror of the defendant's guilt beyond a reasonable doubt, the defense need only confuse one. The joke is not untrue, but it is misleading. If a jury is unable to come to a unanimous verdict, the jury is deemed "hung" and the judge must order a mistrial. Thus, while a mistrial means escape from conviction for the defendant, the escape may only be temporary, as the prosecutor can elect to have a new trial, with a new jury, ordered by the court. I once witnessed a case result in a mistrial two consecutive times before the defendant was found guilty by the third jury.

The number of jurors depends on the charge. In New York, if the top charge is a felony, there are twelve jurors. If the top charge is misdemeanor, there are six jurors. In addition to the twelve or six regular jurors, alternates are usually selected. Alternates hear all of the proof, just like the regular jurors, but do not deliberate unless they are called upon to replace a regular juror. The number of alternates is discretionary, but one or two alternates is the norm. In higher-profile cases or cases where the trial is expected to be lengthy, more alternates may be selected. Many states, like New York, limit the number of alternates.

During the trial, the same as in a bench trial, the judge remains in charge of resolving any disputes over evidence, including which evidence the jury is allowed to consider. The judge also rules on any objections made by the attorneys, including objections over which witness testimony the jury should be allowed to consider. If a witness says something the judge believes should not be considered by the jury, the judge can "strike" the testimony and direct the jury to disregard what it heard.

If you are considering a bench trial, you must rely upon your knowledge of the judge's attitudes and tendencies. But if you are considering a jury trial, you also cannot completely ignore the likely dispositions of the persons who may comprise your jury. While it is certainly much easier to assess one person's disposition than it is to assess the collective disposition of a dozen people, it would be foolish to have your case heard by a jury without at least considering the general attitudes and opinions of the people who will comprise the jury pool. It would be an understatement to say juries are unpredictable. They are. Much more so than judges. Unlike judges, no one jury is ever the same. Defendants and prosecutors pay big bucks to jury consultants, folks who analyze prospective jurors to determine which jurors are most likely to be sympathetic to the interests of other clients.

You do not need to be a jury consultant to analyze potential jurors and achieve at least a basic understanding of the type of people you will have to choose from in selecting a jury. This is one of the few times in life when it is okay to stereotype. Given the process of jury selection, which is discussed in greater detail later on, it is unlikely you are going to know enough about potential jurors to do anything but make raw generalizations. You should have a rudimentary understanding of the basic socioeconomic, racial, and educational backgrounds of the people who live in the area of the state in which your jurors will come from. If your case is in a local court such as a town court, your jury will be comprised of persons residing in the town for which the court sits. If your case is in county court, potential jury members will come from the county for which the court sits.

Jurors are, before anything else, people. They tend to relate to others who share common life experiences and possess similar personal characteristics. If considering a jury trial, you need to ask yourself whether the people who are most likely to sit on your jury will not only understand any defense you intend to raise but can relate to you as a person. If you are a black person accused of committing a crime in a mostly white county, you could face a racist jury pool. If you are accused of stealing in a mostly affluent county, you might face potential jurors who are unable to understand how someone could steal to support his or her family.

When O.J. Simpson was found not guilty, there was consensual shock across the country. People could not believe that, with the amount of evidence against him, any jury could find him not guilty. Upon closer inspection, however, the trial was the perfect case study on the importance of understanding the composition of your jury pool when choosing between a bench trial or a jury trial.

Mr. Simpson was ultimately prosecuted in Los Angeles County in California, a county comprised of a high proportion of minorities, including African-Americans and Hispanics. A centerpiece of Mr. Simpson's defense was race. Mr. Simpson's defense team argued that investigating members of the Los Angeles Police Department were racist, raising questions about their credibility as witnesses for the prosecution. Carrying out that strategy required a jury containing enough people who could understand how a racist police officer could plant evidence and lie to obtain a conviction of an African-American defendant.

As stated earlier, in most criminal cases, the trial occurs in the judicial district where the alleged crime occurs. In New York, if the crime occurred in the city of Rochester, the trial will occur either in the city of Rochester (if a misdemeanor) or the county of Monroe (if a felony), wherein the city of Rochester sits. In the O.J. Simpson case, the alleged murders occurred in Santa Monica, but the prosecutor elected to try the case in the city of Los Angeles. Pundits have long since argued that this was a monumental mistake by the prosecution. Even the infamous Vince Bugliosi, prosecutor of the Charles Manson trial, has said the prosecution's decision to try the case in Los Angeles rather than Santa Monica "dwarfed anything the defense did" in the case.

The high proportion of minorities in the Los Angeles County jury pool allowed Mr. Simpson's defense team to pick a twelve-member jury containing eight African-Americans. Mr. Simpson's defense team understood that it was likely, given the racial composition of the jury pool in Los Angeles County, that the jury would contain enough minorities to allow their strategy to succeed. Had the case remained in Santa Monica County, where the case originally began and where there exists very few minority residents, their strategy may not have been practical.

4

Selecting the Jury

"A jury consists of twelve persons chosen to decide who has the better lawyer."—Robert Frost, American poet

As mentioned in the previous chapter, the O.J. Simpson case is an extreme but relevant case study in how the composition of a jury pool can affect defense strategy and the outcome of a trial. In the O.J. Simpson case, the defense attorneys decided they wanted as many African-Americans on the jury as possible.

The reason for this opinion is that polling had shown, before the trial had even began, that most whites believed O.J. Simpson was guilty, and most African-Americans believed he was innocent. Santa Monica's population was mostly white, and Los Angeles's population was almost 50 percent African-American. It does not take a sociologist to figure out that the defense was more likely to have a more receptive jury pool in Los Angeles than Santa Monica. In fact, when the lawyers arrived at the courthouse on September 24, 1994, to begin selecting the jury, there were 250 prospective jurors in the pool. Of those prospective jurors, only 40 percent of the poll was white, and 28 percent was African-American, far exceeding the proportional composition of African-Americans in Santa Monica. This made it possible for the defense to select eight African-Americans.

Race is just one of many characteristics that might be relevant to your trial. Gender, religious beliefs, sexual orientation, and numerous others can be just as relevant and can influence your trial, depending on the issues anticipated to arise during the trial. Take, for example, gender in the context of the Simpson case. Defense survey data has indicated that female jurors are generally better for the defense than the prosecution. In the Simpson case, a disproportionate number of the jurors were female. Critics have also opined that this was a further mistake made by the prosecution.

The rules that govern how a jury is selected are designed to encourage the selection of jurors who are unbiased and will follow the law and instructions given by the judge. As I stated earlier, picking a jury is really a misnomer. Jury selection is really juror elimination. You get your jury through a process of elimination or de-selection, and both the prosecutor and your attorney do the eliminating. In other words, you do not choose which jurors you want on the jury; you choose which jurors you do not want on the jury.

In selecting your jury, above all else, you want jurors who are unlikely to harbor views that are contrary to the theory of your case. If you are accused of domestic abuse, you need to be careful about allowing jurors to serve who have been victims of domestic abuse. If you are accused of robbing someone, you will probably not want jurors who have been robbed. If one of your defense theories is that the police lied, you probably do not want jurors who have close relatives who are police officers. If you are accused of illegally possessing a firearm, you will probably not want jurors who are against the Second Amendment to the US Constitution, which gives us our right to bear arms.

Venue

Venue refers to where your trial occurs. As I stated already, criminal charges are filed, and any trial ultimately occurs, where the alleged crime occurred. And as I have also illustrated using the O.J. Simpson case as an example, where a trial occurs can have a significant impact on the trial itself. In New York, if the alleged crime occurred within 500 yards of a county's boundary, the case can be tried in that county.

Despite the rules of venue, you can request that the court move the case to another county if you can demonstrate that you cannot receive a fair and impartial trial in the present venue. Change of venue motions are rarely granted prior to jury selection. It is more common that the issue of fairness becomes apparent after jury selection begins. Cases warranting change of venue are usually higher-profile cases garnering a lot of outside media attention. However, the mere fact that a large proportion of prospective jurors have heard something about the case before trial is usually not enough. To convince a judge to change venue, you must prove not only that there has been extensive publicity, but that that publicity has aroused deep resentment and passion in the county where the trial is to be held.

Voir Dire

The process of picking a jury is called jury selection or voir dire, (pronounced vwahr, with a near silent "r," deer). Voir dire is derived from the French term "to see to speak." The English term is a legal phrase that refers to a variety of procedures that occur during a trial, one of which is the preliminary examination of prospective jurors to determine their qualifications and suitability to serve on the jury. The examination of the prospective jurors is conducted by either your attorney or the judge, depending on whether your trial is in state court or federal court. In state courts, the attorney is allowed to speak with and question prospective jurors directly, while in most federal courts, the judge normally does all of the speaking.

I find this distinction not to be an irrelevant one. Judges doing the examination of potential jurors, for the most part, merely read questions that are designed to get the potential jurors to agree with the law. To the contrary, lawyers' questioning is, or at least should be, designed to get prospective jurors to reveal things about themselves. This point is perfectly illustrated by a story I once heard from another attorney. The attorney was describing a trial he had in federal court. On the first day of jury selection, the judge allowed the attorneys to examine fifty of the prospective jurors sitting in the pool. Following their examination, approximately half of fifty prospective jurors were eliminated for cause—that is, they were eliminated without the attorneys having to use one of their peremptory challenges because it was determined that they could not be fair to one side or the other. The judge then brought in another approximately fifty jurors for examination. This time, the judge examined them conventionally by personally questioning them. Following the judge's questioning, only a few jurors were eliminated for cause.

The difference was how the prospective jurors were examined. The attorneys did not just ask boilerplate questions such as, "Will you follow the law as given to you?" or "If the defendant chooses not to testify, do you promise not to infer guilt?" Instead, the attorneys asked open-ended questions, questions that encouraged the prospective jurors to give their opinions and not just agree or disagree with the judge. The proof was in the pudding.

If you face a trial in federal court, it is important that your attorney request that the court give him or her the opportunity to personally examine the prospective jurors. Usually, the judge will at least allow the attorneys to submit proposed questions to the judge for introduction to the prospective jurors. The judge will take the questions proposed by the prosecutor and your attorney and choose which ones to ask the prospective jurors. However, even this has significant limitations. When the judge asks the questions, you lose any opportunity to follow up the answers, and the judge will often change the wording of the question, take it out of context, or forget to ask it altogether.

Regardless of whether you are in state court or federal court, the basic routine is the same. Before trial begins, the court sends out notices to eligible jurors directing them to show up on the date of trial. As stated previously, if you are in a local state court, the notices get sent out to residents of the town or city in which the court sits. If you are in a superior court, like a county court, the notices get sent out to residents of the county in which the court sits. Thus, if your case is in Monroe County Court in the state of New York, only residents of Monroe County are eligible to serve on your jury. In federal court, prospective jurors come from a wider geographic range, a range usually encompassing several counties or districts. This is one of the reasons plaintiff's attorneys in civil cases often choose federal court over state court; it usually guarantees a broader cross-section of people from which to select the jury. In a federal criminal case, it is much less likely that the selected jury will be influenced by local biases and attitudes.

Everyone who responds to a notice will arrive at the courthouse on the given date and time. Everyone who responds constitutes the jury pool from which the jury will ultimately be selected. Trial begins by the judge randomly selecting a predetermined number of potential jurors for questioning by the judge and, if in state court, the attorneys. In a typical trial, the jury pool will fill up the gallery to the courtroom. The court will have the name of each member of the pool written down on a form and will pick out the predetermined number of names anonymously from a hat or, in some cases, an old-fashioned bingo cage. Most judges select either fourteen or twenty-one names at a time.

As names are called, the selected prospective jurors will fill a seat somewhere near the judge and attorneys, usually in and around the jury box if the courtroom has one. I like to use a prepared chart that has enough boxes for every name called. As a name is called, I write the name of the prospective juror in his or her own box, with room in the box to add notes later on. I also bring with me enough copies so I can provide my client with his or her own copy to use during the selection process. If your attorney does not provide you with something similar, I recommend that you draw your own on a piece of paper. It does not have to be artful, just something that allows you to remember the names of the prospective jurors, along with any notes that will help you later when it comes time to eliminate prospective jurors.

Once the first fourteen or twenty-one names are called, the judge will usually ask them certain standard questions designed to eliminate any obviously unqualified jurors, such as jurors with physical or mental problems that would prevent them from offering further service. Some judges use a standard questionnaire containing these questions. Standard questions include questions about the prospective jurors' occupations, relationship to law enforcement or court officials, hobbies, whether they or a family member have ever been a victim of a crime, whether they have served on a jury before, and whether there is anything they believe would prevent them from being fair and impartial, which is the most fundamental requirement of being a juror. Usually, the judge's initial round of questions will thin out the herd. If prospective jurors are released by the judge before the attorneys begin their own questioning, the judge may choose to fill the empty spots immediately by calling out new names.

After the judge has finished, the prosecutor is given the first opportunity to speak with the panel. The judge will usually give both the prosecutor and your attorney a set time limit. A normal time limit is around twenty minutes. The prosecutor goes first, followed by your attorney.

Good voir dire is a skill learned and honed though experience, and not every prosecutor and defense attorney is equally adept. It is the only time during the trial that your attorney is allowed to directly speak with the jury, and it is an opportunity to not only learn which prospective jurors you do not want on the jury, but to build rapport with those whom you want on the jury. It is about self-education and education of the prospective jurors about the legal and factual issues that are likely to arise during the trial. For example, if you are charged with DWI, your attorney may wish to spend some time letting the prospective jurors know that it is not unlawful to drink and drive; it is only unlawful to drive when you have drunk too much (alcohol, that is). I have had DWI trials where prospective jurors have told me, candidly, that they believe it should be unlawful to drive after having anything to drink. Obviously, I did not allow those jurors to be selected.

The exact questions to ask the prospective jurors will differ from case to case. They will be largely dependent on the issues and subject matters anticipated to be at the center of the trial. Many general questions, such as questions concerning hobbies and background, will be included on the general questionnaire, if one is used by the court, or as part of the judge's own questioning. I recommend that you write down some questions you think might be appropriate before the trial and give them to your attorney. It is up to your attorney what, if any of the questions, to use, but you might think of something your attorney did not think of. I always welcome my clients' input, and I have often used questions and ideas for questions presented by my clients. As I previously explained, the type of questions that can be asked are limitless. For illustration purposes, I have included a few examples below.

1. If you were my client, would you want you to be a juror in this case?
2. Do you believe defendants should testify at trial? And if my client does not testify, what will you think?
3. Do you believe police officers always tell the truth?
4. What kind of things do you look for in determining whether someone is telling the truth?
5. Do you believe the burden of proof at trial is too heavy?

The process, if done effectively, is more of a discussion between the prospective jurors and the attorney than just a question-and-answer session. The key is to get the prospective jurors to speak as much as possible and to share as much about themselves as possible, both with your attorney and, if possible, among themselves. Questions that encourage prospective jurors to open up, as opposed to giving "yes" or "no" answers, are preferable. There are few restrictions on what the prosecutor and defense attorney can talk about with the prospective jurors. Pretty much any topic is fair game. Although, it is generally a good idea not to offend anyone who could end up on the jury. Most judges will allow your attorney to give prospective jurors the option of speaking privately at the bench if there is something a prospective juror does not wish to share in front of everyone.

While all of this is happening, you should be recording things on your chart about the prospective jurors, including things they say that you believe are noteworthy. I believe this might be the one part of the trial process where you can help your attorney the most. Your attorney should be more focused on listening to the prospective jurors and asking appropriate follow-up questions than writing down every response. If your attorney is writing too much, he is probably not listening enough. In larger criminal cases, I like to have co-counsel take down the responses, but if I do not have co-counsel, I rely upon my client to assist. For example, if prospective juror Bill Smith says he thinks that most defendants are guilty because the police arrested them, you will probably want to remember what he said. Or, maybe a prospective juror has three brothers who work for the police department that arrested you. If your attorney is competent, he will be doing the same thing. Your attorney must ultimately make the final call on which prospective jurors to eliminate, but you should have input into the decision process. If you have a bad feeling about a particular prospective juror, you should let your attorney know. I always appreciate my client's input, and I often rely upon it when I am torn on a particular prospective juror.

I highly recommend that you take good notes of, not only what you hear, but what you see. Often, non-verbal cues are more important than what the prospective jurors say. As the old saying goes, the eyes do not lie. Watch how a prospective juror makes a statement. Also, watch the expressions and gestures of prospective jurors who are not speaking. If prospective juror Bill Smith says he thinks you should not be allowed to operate a motor vehicle if you have had anything to drink, watch for other prospective jurors nodding their heads in agreement. Bottom line, pay close attention to everything. Your attorney has only two eyes and two ears, and he or she is unlikely to see and hear everything.

Challenge Prospective Jurors

As I said earlier, selecting or picking a jury is really a misnomer. Juries are arrived at by process of elimination or a process of de-selection. There are two ways to eliminate a prospective juror. The first is by challenging the juror for cause, and the second is using what is called a peremptory challenge. There is no limitation on how many prospective jurors your attorney can challenge for cause. Any prospective juror who, in the opinion of the judge, cannot be fair, unbiased, or capable of serving as a juror can be eliminated for cause. The judge can even eliminate a prospective juror himself without consulting with the attorneys if the judge believes it is clear that the prospective juror is unqualified to serve. A judge can also dismiss a prospective juror who is unable to serve due to the time commitment. This last issue comes up more than you might think. Many prospective jurors have jobs or cgukdreb to care for or a vacation planned. Even if the judge will not dismiss a prospective juror because of another time commitment, you may not want someone on your jury who might be distracted or inclined to rush his or her deliberations because he or she is falling behind at work or has children that will not have someone to watch them.

The most obvious basis for eliminating a prospective juror for cause is a person who has indicated that he or she cannot be fair to one side or the other. An example would be Mr. Smith, who said he thought any defendant is probably guilty because he or she was arrested. Or Mr. Johnson, who remarked that all police were corrupt, and he would not be able to believe anything they said at trial. If the prospective juror says he or she cannot or he or she cannot be sure, the judge should dismiss the prospective juror for cause. Ultimately, the issue for the judge is whether the judge believes the challenged person's state of mind is likely to preclude that juror from rendering an impartial verdict based upon the evidence likely to be adduced at trial. If the judge believes the juror is unlikely to remain fair, the judge should dismiss the juror for cause.

Prospective jurors can also be dismissed for cause because they suffer from a physical ailment that would prohibit them from listening, seeing, or even just being able to sit in one spot for long stretches of time. During a recent jury trial, I had a prospective juror fall asleep on me during jury selection. I have also had prospective jurors who could not hear me because of hearing loss, prospective jurors who did not speak English, and prospective jurors who were too blind to distinguish me from my client. Needless to say, all of those prospective jurors were appropriately dismissed for cause.

Whenever an issue regarding a juror's ability to be fair and impartial arises, the prospective juror must, to survive a challenge for cause, state in unequivocal terms that his prior state of mind will not influence his deliberations, and he will render a verdict based solely on the evidence adduced at trial. These terms must be stated with conviction. And even if the prospective juror states confidently that he or she can be fair, but his or her body language belies the words, the judge can dismiss the prospective juror for cause. Judges like to ask a prospective juror who has expressed an inability to be fair as a result of some past experience whether that prospective juror could put those past experiences in the proverbial bottle and cork it. Prospective jurors often like to say things like, "I think I can be fair" or "I will try to be fair." If a prospective juror says something along those lines, he should be challenged for cause and dismissed. In some cases, however, like when the prospective juror's viewpoints could be slanted in your favor, your attorney should try to "rehabilitate" the prospective juror by getting the prospective juror to state that he can be fair.

Unlike challenges for cause, your attorney does not need the judge to approve a peremptory challenge. Peremptory challenges are like trump cards. You can use one on any prospective juror you wish, as long as it is not for a discriminatory reason such as race or gender. However, unlike challenges for cause, you only have a limited number of peremptory challenges to use. The exact number of challenges depends on the seriousness of the top charge against you. For example, if you are charged with a class A felony, the most serious charge possible in New York, you are allowed to use twenty peremptory challenges. If you are charged with a class B or C felony, you have fifteen challenges. With any other felony, you are given ten challenges. If the top charge is only a misdemeanor, you get three challenges.

Once you have selected the required number of jurors, you will also receive two additional challenges for each alternate juror. As stated earlier, the selection of alternate jurors is left to the discretion of the judge, with one exception, that no more than six alternate jurors can be selected. In a typical twelve-juror trial, the court will generally ask that the parties select two alternate jurors.

Alternate jurors are like pinch-hitters in a baseball game. They sit with the regular jurors during the trial and listen to all of the evidence presented. While the trial is ongoing, they act no differently than the regular jurors. If one of the regular jurors is unable, for whatever reason, to finish his or her duty while evidence is still being presented, the first selected alternate can take that juror's place. If the court believes a juror is grossly unqualified, such as when the juror is unable to stay awake during the evidence, the court can dismiss the juror and replace him or her with an alternate juror without your consent. However, if the court does not believe the juror is grossly unqualified, you must consent to replacing the juror with an alternate.

Once all of the evidence has been presented and the jury begins its deliberation, the alternate jurors do not deliberate with the regular jurors.

They are separated from the regular jurors in a separate room and do not discuss the case with the regular jurors. If something happens that results in one of the jurors becoming unable to finish deliberations, such as illness or a family emergency, an alternate juror can take that juror's spot in the deliberation room. However, unlike substitution before the jurors begin their deliberations, a juror can only be substituted with an alternate if you consent, in writing.

In some cases, your attorney may also have legal grounds to challenge the entire panel of prospective jurors. Challenging the panel is commonly done when it can be shown that a substantial and identifiable segment of the community is not included in the pool, and this was the result of a process that systematically excluded the group. For example, if you are being prosecuted in a county where African-Americans make up 50 percent of the total population, and there are no African-Americans in the jury pool, your attorney may seek to challenge the pool by demonstrating the disparity between the proportion of African-Americans in the county and in the jury pool.

After all of the prospective jurors have been appropriately examined by the judge, the prosecutor, and your attorney, the judge will meet with the prosecutor and your attorney to begin the actual process of selecting jury members. This process is done outside the presence of the jury pool, usually in the jury room. Sometimes, the judge will conduct selection at the judge's bench right inside the courtroom. Wherever it is held, it cannot be done in front of the prospective jurors. They should not be aware of which side is eliminating which prospective jurors. You have the right to attend this meeting with your attorney. At the very least, before the meeting, I suggest that your attorney ask the judge for permission to meet with you privately to review your notes and gain any input you may have regarding prospective jurors.

The selection process begins with the prosecutor challenging prospective jurors for cause. If the prosecutor makes a challenge for cause, your attorney can either stipulate to the removal of the challenged prospective juror or submit his or her argument against the challenge. If there is a disagreement over the challenged juror, the judge will make the final decision. After the prosecutor has made his challenges for cause, your attorney then has the opportunity to make challenges for cause.

After challenges for cause are made, peremptory challenges are made. Again, the prosecutor challenges first, followed by your attorney. When challenging for either cause or using a peremptory challenge, the number of prospective jurors to be considered will depend on the number of jurors still needed to be selected. For example, when beginning the selection process, if twelve regular jurors are needed, you will begin by considering prospective jurors one through twelve.

Once all of the jurors, including alternates, are selected, the judge will swear in the jury by requiring them to give an oath. This is a critical moment, because it usually represents your last chance to plead guilty. Once the jury is sworn in by the judge, you can no longer plead guilty.

5

The Trial: Opening Argument to Verdict

"Whoever tells the best story wins." —John Quincy Adams

Defense Strategy

For my client John, who was charged with manslaughter, arising out of a bar fight, our defense strategy was straightforward: self-defense. In the O.J. Simpson case, the overall strategy was to demonstrate that law enforcement fabricated evidence motivated by racism. You and your attorney should develop a defense strategy well before you walk into the courtroom on the first day of trial. Defense strategy will dictate everything from the type of juror you want on your jury, to how you go about cross-examining prosecution witnesses, to which witnesses, if any, you elect to put on the stand in your defense and whether you testify. Defense strategy is not static; it can, and often will, evolve over the course of the trial, and it is important to be flexible, to go with the flow. But by the time trial comes around, you and your attorney should have a basic strategy outlined, including a plan for setting that strategy in motion.

Choosing which defense strategy or strategies to employ is ultimately the call of your attorney. You have a right to suggest strategies to your attorney, and you should be kept apprised of your attorney's intentions on strategy, but your attorney is within the bounds of ethics to make decisions on strategy, including which witnesses to put on the stand, which evidence to present to the jury, and what arguments to make to the jury. Clients are often under the misimpression that I am like a racehorse, my movements dictated by the client's tug and pulls on the reins. There are many decisions that are solely the client's to make, including whether to testify at trial and whether to testify before the grand jury, to name two of the most fundamental of rights. But not only is it your attorney's right to make the final calls on matters of strategy, you should encourage it. You are probably not an attorney. And even if you are, you are too emotionally involved in the case to make the objective decisions that are required to present an effective defense. So I cannot urge you enough to place your faith in your attorney, and if you cannot do so with the attorney you have, do everything possible to obtain one with whom you can.

The best strategies are usually straightforward. Some cases may warrant multiple defenses. It is not necessary, even, that all of those defenses are consistent. For example, where you are accused of selling drugs, it is not unusual to both deny the sale and theorize that the police entrapped you. While there are cases where multiple and/or inconsistent defenses are warranted, doing so comes with risk. Presenting multiple/inconsistent defenses can confuse the jury and undermine your credibility. Prosecutors like to stress this credibility problem to the jury, referring to it as riding two horses into battle.

I recently faced this dilemma in a marijuana possession case. My client was charged with possessing eight or more ounces of marijuana. The marijuana was found by the police in a vehicle containing my client and one passenger. There was a total of nine ounces inside the car. Approximately two ounces of marijuana was found on my client. Another two ounces was found in a bag by my client's feet. The remaining five ounces was found in a bag held by the passenger. Our defense theory was that my client possessed marijuana but only the marijuana found on my client and in the bag on the floor by his feet. Thus, under our theory, he only possessed four ounces, not the eight ounces required to convict him of the charged crime.

It is important to remember that your attorney has an ethical obligation not to advise, encourage, or induce you or a witness to lie on the stand. This is known as suborning perjury. Those ethical rules provide that, if an attorney knows you or another witness called by you will lie on the stand, that attorney must take certain steps to prevent it, including possibly having to withdraw as your attorney in the case. This is the primary reason why most attorneys will not ask, and do not wish to know, whether you committed the subject crime. This can raise an interesting ethical dilemma for your attorney, since your attorney also owes you an ethical obligation to advocate zealously on your behalf, which most clients assume means the attorney must be willing to do almost anything that will give them a better chance of being acquitted.

The point is that if you or your witness intend to offer, as fact, anything that is not truthful, it is best that you do not let your attorney know about it. Now, that having been said, let me say to you that I do *not* advise that you lie to your attorney. While it might earn you some advantage in the case, it is even more likely that it will turn out to be disadvantageous. I could write a separate chapter in this book on the amount of times I have reached trial only to find out, for the first time, that something my client claimed to be true was not, or to find out something my client knew but chose not to tell me. These situations are usually devastating for the client, as the attorney is left with his proverbial "pants down." Depending on the significance of the fact, it could mean your defense theory of the case could crash and burn before your very eyes, ruining both the credibility of you and your attorney. In the end, juries just want the truth. If they believe you, your attorney, or a witness called to testify on your behalf is being dishonest or is trying to hide something from them, they will sense it, and it will be reflected adversely in their verdict.

No defendant in a criminal case has any obligation to present a defense, as you are presumed innocent. However, in formulating a cohesive defense strategy in your case, there are two ways you can present a defense. The first way is to discredit the prosecutor's theory through some combination of cross-examining the prosecution's witnesses and putting on your own witnesses. The burden of proof remains on the prosecution to prove your guilt beyond a reasonable doubt. The second way of offering a defense is through the use of an affirmative defense. I will discuss affirmative defenses at greater length later in the chapter. But in general, an affirmative defense is a defense you have the burden of proving.

Opening Statement

By admitting to possessing some of the marijuana, my client risked the jury thinking, "In for an inch, in for a mile." Or in for one ounce, in for eight. Whatever theory or defense you choose, your first chance to introduce it to the jury comes during your attorney's opening statement. Both the prosecutor and your attorney can give an opening statement. An opening statement is required by the prosecutor. Your attorney is not required to give an opening statement, but it is highly recommended that he or she does. Assuming both the prosecutor and your attorney give an opening statement, the prosecutor goes first, followed by your attorney (the order is reversed for closing summations, which will be discussed later). In some states, including New York, your attorney can request that he or she be allowed to make the opening statement after the prosecution has presented all of its proof. Whether to permit this is up to the judge, and it is rarely granted.

Once the jury is selected, there are only two remaining opportunities to speak directly to the jurors: the opening statement and the closing summation. The opening statement is your attorney's chance to tell the jury what he or she expects the jury will hear and see during the trial and what he or she expects the jury will not hear and see during the trial. The judge will instruct the jury that nothing that is said by your attorney or the prosecutor during opening statements is evidence. The judge will also instruct the jury that your attorney is not obligated to give an opening statement.

Assuming your attorney elects to give an opening statement, he or she should be careful not to make any promises that will not be fulfilled during the trial. For example, if your attorney tells the jury that a particular witness will say something on the stand, he or she should be reasonably sure the witness will, in fact, do so. If there are any doubts about what a particular witness will say or what a particular piece of evidence will show during the trial, it is usually better to just leave it alone during the opening statement rather than risk losing face with the jury.

The same is true for the prosecutor. The prosecutor's opening statement should describe the nature of the charges against you and lay out the evidence that is expected to prove the charges. The prosecutor cannot intentionally refer to evidence that he or she knows will not be presented during the trial, and if he or she does so, this can be grounds for an appeal if you are ultimately convicted. This does not mean every piece of evidence referred to by the prosecutor must be presented at trial, but all representations made by the prosecutor during his or her opening statement must be made in good faith.

I recommend that you write down everything the prosecutor says he or she will prove during his or her opening statement. If the prosecutor says something you know cannot be proven during the trial, your attorney can point out this fact during his or her opening statement. Even more importantly, if the prosecutor promises evidence that is not presented during the trial, your attorney can stress this failure at the end of the trial during his or her summation. For example, if the prosecutor says the proof will show that you were wearing a blue jacket and brown pants when you committed the alleged crime, but witnesses during the trial say you were wearing a red jacket and blue jeans, your attorney should stress this discrepancy to the jury during his or her closing argument.

The opening statement is your attorney's chance to paint a picture for the jury or, more useful, a roadmap of the proof he expects the jury will hear and see. Good opening statements enable the jurors to see the case from your perspective, making them feel, see, and hear the things you would have, rather than the jurors just looking on as an outside observer. This is part of the overall goal of getting the jurors to relate to you as a person and not just a defendant accused of some crime. Your attorney cannot expressly ask the jurors to put themselves in "your shoes." However, jurors will be placed in your shoes if the opening statement is done right.

I also believe that good opening statements should not ignore the problem areas of your case. Almost every case has some fact or issue that is not positive. Keeping in line with my earlier advice of being truthful with the jury, I believe your attorney should choose to, rather than ignore those problem areas, meet them head-on. Any sting brought on by the adverse evidence will be at least mitigated by mentioning it and portraying it in the best possible light. And the jury will appreciate your attorney's candor and honesty. Remember, the credibility of your attorney equals the credibility of you. In cases where you do not testify, the voice of your attorney will be the only voice the jury hears, so it is critical that your attorney take great precautions to ensure his credibility, and by extension, your credibility, is upheld.

People's Case in Chief

After opening statements are complete, the people, represented by the prosecutor, usually an assistant district attorney, except in small counties or, in the extremely high-profile case, where the actual district attorney will assume the role, begins presentation of the case in chief. The case in chief is where the prosecutor puts on all of the evidence he or she intends to present to the jury. The evidence the prosecutor presents must be presented through witnesses, unless the prosecutor and your attorney stipulate to a piece of evidence without the necessity of a witness.

Before the trial begins, the court will usually require that each side declare which witnesses each side intends to call to testify. Thus, usually you will know, before trial begins, who the prosecutor intends to call to the stand, which will allow you and your attorney to properly prepare. The prosecutor will usually start by putting the police officers who were first to the scene of the incident, followed by the officers who made the arrest, if they are different. Remember, the prosecutor is also attempting to paint a picture for the jury, and he or she will usually attempt to do so by presenting facts in a chronological order.

Witnesses can usually only testify about any facts to which they have direct knowledge. For example, witnesses generally cannot mention statements made by other people, as those statements normally constitute hearsay. There are some exceptions to this "hearsay rule," such as statements made by you. As witnesses testify, your attorney can make objections to any questions or responses that violate the rules of evidence. There are numerous rules of evidence and numerous objections your attorney can make. You should not be expected to know all of them; that is why you are represented by an attorney. But here are some of the more frequently made objections:

1. Testimony not relevant (A witness's testimony must always be relevant to some issue at trial.)
2. Question calls for hearsay
3. Leading question (The side that calls the witness questions the witness first during what is called "direct examination." During direct examination, the questioning attorney is not allowed to "lead the witness." For example, if the prosecutor wishes to ask the witness what color the light was, he must ask, "What color was the light?" He cannot ask, "Was the light red?" or "The light was red, wasn't it?"
4. Question was already asked and answered
5. Question calls for speculation or witness is speculating (This relates to the rule that a witness cannot ordinarily testify regarding things to which he or she does not have direct knowledge.)
6. Answer is non-responsive to the question
7. Lack of foundation (Before any evidence may be considered by the jury, including testimonial evidence, a proper foundation must be established. For example, before the prosecutor can ask a police officer what you were wearing, he must first establish that the police officer actually saw you.)

You should listen closely to what the witness says during direct examination, as the witness could say something that either you know to be untrue, or you know something that could cast some doubt in the jury's mind. If you have something you think might be helpful to your attorney, I recommend writing it down for your attorney to see after the witness finishes testifying. I do not recommend whispering in your attorney's ear during the testimony, as it could distract your attorney from listening to everything the witness says. As important as it might be for you to communicate with your attorney, it is even more important that your attorney hear everything the prosecutor asks and the witness says. Interfering with your attorney's attention could result in a missed objection or a missed cross-examination opportunity.

There are basically two types of witnesses the prosecutor can put on the stand: fact witnesses and expert witnesses. Fact witnesses or non-expert witnesses must testify regarding things to which they have personal knowledge and are generally prohibited from giving opinions on matters. Fact witnesses constitute the majority of witnesses that are called to testify during trial. In the criminal trial, police officers are the most common type of fact witnesses. However, in certain instances, assuming the proper foundation is set, police officers are allowed to give opinions without being called as an expert. For example, in a DWI case, police officers are allowed, once it is established that they have received sufficient training, to opine whether the defendant has passed or failed field sobriety tests, whether the defendant had consumed alcohol, and whether, based on that consumption, the defendant was able to operate his or her vehicle in a reasonable and prudent manner.

An expert witness is a witness who, by virtue of his or her training, education, and/or experience, has a specialized knowledge about a particular subject matter. Common experts include experts on DNA, blood splatter (like the character Dexter in the hit television show "Dexter"), psychology, computer forensics, fingerprints, and ballistics. Before an expert witness is allowed to give an opinion, it must be first established that the witness is, in fact, an expert on the subject about which the expert intends to testify. This is called establishing a foundation, and it is usually done by eliciting from the expert the basis for the expert's knowledge. In other words, what makes that witness qualified to give such an opinion. For example, in a DWI case, it is not uncommon for the defense to call an expert on extrapolation, which involves giving an opinion on what the defendant's BAC was at an earlier point in time based on numerous factors. Before such an expert can give his or opinion, your attorney will typically ask questions that elicit the expert's relevant education, employment, training, and real-world experience as it relates to measuring a person's BAC. Once that foundation is laid, the witness can then proceed to give opinions on the defendant's BAC.

After the prosecutor finishes his direct examination of a witness, your attorney then has the opportunity to conduct what is called cross-examination. Cross-examination is your attorney's chance to question the prosecutor's witness and, hopefully, discredit that witness's testimony and support your defense theory, including any affirmative defenses you may have. Unlike during direct examination, your attorney is not obligated to ask non-leading questions. In fact, good cross-examination involves the use of mostly leading questions. During cross-examination, your attorney will usually ask questions designed to elicit "yes" or "no" answers. For example, by asking, "The light was red, correct?" the witness must either confirm or deny that the light was red, unless the witness does not know the answer.

In most states, cross-examination is not allowed to exceed the scope of direct examination. In other words, questioning of the witness during cross-examination is limited to the subjects or issues covered during direct examination. There are exceptions to this general rule, such as questioning that might exceed the scope but is intended to impeach the witness's credibility.

Like my recommendation that you take notes during the witness's direct examination, I recommend that you take notes during cross-examination. After I finish cross-examining a witness, I will sometimes confer briefly with my client to see if there is anything my client thinks I missed. That does not mean your attorney will or should utilize your input. The decision of whether to do so should be left to the discretion of your attorney. You should, however, expect that your attorney will listen to your suggestions, if given at an appropriate time during the trial.

An effective cross-examination begins before the witness even takes the stand. It begins with preparation, knowing everything there is to know about the witness, including every statement that witness has ever made and everything about the witness's background. There are limits to what your attorney can find out about a witness himself. I strongly recommend that you authorize your attorney to hire a private investigator to speak with non-law enforcement prosecution witnesses and conduct background checks on them. Most attorney retainer agreements will not cover this expense, but the additional expense is invaluable. Some background checks can be conducted by your attorney or even you, but there is no substitute to having a private investigator speak with witnesses before trial begins. The private investigator should reach out to every possible witness, including witnesses you intend to call as a witness at trial. Witnesses are not obligated to speak with the private investigator, and most will not do so. For those who will speak, the private investigator should be looking for discrepancies between their current statement and any statements made to police, as well as leads to additional evidence, including other witnesses who could possess information helpful to your defense.

I also strongly recommend that you share everything you know about all possible witnesses with your attorney before trial, no matter how big or small it may seem at the time. Let your attorney determine the importance of what you know. Something that seems insignificant to you could turn out to be crucial come trial.

When cross-examination is complete, the prosecutor has the right to conduct re-direct examination of his or her witnesses. Re-direct examination must stay within the scope of your attorney's cross-examination, just like your attorney had to stay within the scope of the prosecutor's direct examination. This back-and-forth can, in theory, and in the discretion of the judge, go on indefinitely; re-direct leads to re-cross, which can lead to re-re-cross, etc.

Trial Order of Dismissal/Motion to Dismiss

After the prosecutor has presented all of the witnesses he or she intends to call to the stand, the people's case in chief is deemed complete. This also means the prosecutor cannot, with a few exceptions that are mentioned below, present any further evidence against you.

Once the case in chief is complete, your attorney can now ask the judge to dismiss the charges against you without the case ever going to the jury or judge later for decision. In New York, your attorney makes a motion for a trial order of dismissal. Some states may simply call it a motion to dismiss or something similar. Usually the motion is made orally on the record and outside the presence of the jury. However, in some cases, although very rare, the judge may give your attorney the opportunity to submit a written motion.

The standard on a motion for a trial order of dismissal is much less forgiving than the beyond a reasonable doubt standard that is used to arrive at a verdict. On a motion for a trial order of dismissal, the judge must, looking at all of the evidence in the light most favorable to the prosecution, determine whether the people have established a *prima facie* case or, in layman's terms, presented enough evidence to conceivably establish all of the elements of the charges against you or some lesser included charge.

The judge can either decide the motion on the spot or reserve his or her decision until later, even after a verdict has already been reached. Do not get your hopes up too high. These motions are rarely granted. I, for example, have never had this motion granted in a felony jury trial, and I have had cases where I genuinely believed granting the motion was warranted. The simple truth is that most judges, as the politically elected human beings they are, are highly reluctant to dismiss a case on his or her own. Especially in jury trials, it is simply much easier and safer to let the jury make the decision.

Defense Case

After your attorney makes the motion, you have the opportunity to present your own case. Keeping in mind that the burden of proof always remains with the people, and you are presumed innocent until proven guilty beyond a reasonable doubt, you have no obligation to put on your own case. In fact, in the typical criminal case, it is common not to put on a defense case, which means it is common to not put on any of your own witnesses. If you do not intend to present any evidence, your attorney will simply stand up and announce to the court, "Your honor, the defense rests." If you do intend to present some evidence, your attorney will call to the stand your first witness.

In addition to yourself as a witness, which I will discuss further shortly, there are four basic types of witnesses your attorney may consider putting on the stand: (1) the rebuttal witness, (2) the impeachment witness, (3) the expert witness, and (4) the character witness. Not each witness will necessarily be exclusive of each other. For example, one particular witness might be called to serve as a rebuttal witness and an impeachment witness.

The rebuttal witness is a witness whose purpose is to contradict the testimony of a witness called by the people during their case in chief. For example, say a police officer testifies that the weather at the time you were pulled over for DWI was warm and dry, when you know the weather was cold and snowing. During your defense case, your attorney could put on the stand a witness to rebut the police officer's testimony by testifying that the weather was not warm and dry.

An impeachment witness is similar to the rebuttal witness. The difference is how the witness is used. The rebuttal witness is used to present a contradictory fact or set of facts. An impeachment witness is used to directly challenge or call into question the credibility of another witness. Here is a common scenario: The alleged victim to an assault testifies at trial that your client was wearing a powder blue leisure suit when he assaulted him. However, a month before the trial, your attorney had sent a private investigator to speak with the victim, and the victim told him your client was wearing a black tuxedo. At trial, your attorney would put on the private investigator, as an impeachment witness, to testify regarding what the victim told him.

The expert witness serves the same purpose for you as he or she does for the people during their case. Subject to the evidentiary rules requiring that the proper foundation be set, an expert witness provides you with an opportunity to give the judge or jury testimony from a person who has specialized knowledge and is generally thought not to have a bias for one side or the other. Juries tend to find experts, particularly medical experts, more credible than fact witnesses, who are usually associated with the side that has called the witness. Of course, expert witnesses are expensive, usually requiring exorbitant fees to give their opinion and even more exorbitant fees to testify at trial. Thus, it is just not always practical to hire an expert, even when one might be beneficial to your defense.

Finally, the character witness. The purpose of the character witness is precisely what the name suggests, to present evidence of another person's character, usually either your character or the character of the alleged victim. Most states, like New York, have strict rules governing the type of character evidence that can be presented through a character witness. Generally, evidence of character cannot be presented solely for the purpose of proving you or the victim acted in accordance with a particular character trait. Given the numerous rules limiting the use of character evidence, witnesses whose sole purpose is introducing evidence of character are seldom used, but when the evidence is admitted for the judge or jury's consideration, it can be extremely effective. I recently defended a client against a charge of conspiracy to possess and sell cocaine. His alleged role in the conspiracy was as a translator for another conspirator, who happened to be his uncle. Specifically, it was alleged that he used his ability to speak both English and Spanish to translate several telephone calls between his uncle, who could only speak Spanish, and another individual, who could only speak English.

The subject calls were recorded, so there was no denying that he did the translating. However, there was some question regarding whether he understood that his translation of the subject calls was helping his uncle sell cocaine. Neither his uncle nor the other individual expressly spoke about selling cocaine. Further, my client was mentally handicapped. In our defense case, in addition to an expert witness that testified regarding my client's mental handicap, we put on my client's father and a friend to testify regarding his character. His father and friend testified that he had a reputation for being willing to help anyone out without questioning the motive. The judge allowed the testimony to be heard by the jury, and the hope was that the jury would believe he was capable of lending a hand to his uncle without necessarily intending to facilitate a drug deal.

Should I Testify?

One of the most difficult decisions you must make in your trial is whether to testify. Unlike most other decisions that must be made during the course of a trial, the decision of whether to testify is wholly your own and cannot be made by your attorney. You have a constitutional right to testify in your defense at trial. Your attorney should advise you of his or her opinion on the matter, but the final call is yours and yours alone. Before it is even your turn to testify, the judge will ask you and your attorney if you intend to testify, which should be done outside the presence of the jury. The judge will remind you that it is your right to testify and will ask that you state, for the record, whether you have had enough time to discuss this issue with your attorney and what is your decision. While things can happen during the course of a trial that may affect your decision on whether to testify, before trial even begins, you should spend time with your attorney discussing this issue, and you should already have a good idea of whether you will testify. And even if you have decided before trial that you will not testify, you should go over potential testimony with your attorney so you are prepared in the event that decision changes. Prepare for every possible contingency.

If you do not testify, the court, upon the request of your attorney, will instruct the jury that you have no obligation to testify, and the jury cannot infer guilt from your decision not to testify. However, the reality is that some jurors will take your decision not to testify as a sign of guilt. Some jurors believe that a person with nothing to hide would never give up the opportunity to speak directly to the jury.

Despite this reality, I have found that, in most cases, testifying on your own behalf at trial is simply too risky. If I had to estimate the number of times I have recommended to a client that he or she testify at trial, I would probably put that number at about 25 percent. When I do make the recommendation, it is usually either because I believe the jury is leaning towards a guilty verdict and I think the client's testimony might reverse the tide, or where the only witnesses to the alleged crime are the victim and the defendant, and I think the jury has found the victim's testimony credible.

The only time it is really mandatory that you testify is when you have raised and wish to pursue at trial an affirmative defense, such as duress. An affirmative defense is a defense the defendant has the burden of proving at trial. It is often referred to as an "excuse defense" because the defendant does not deny the charged conduct. Rather, the defendant argues that he or she should not be held criminally responsible for the conduct because of some excuse. While the overall burden of proving the defendant's guilt always remains on the prosecution, the burden of proving an affirmative defense rests on the defendant.

The one affirmative defense most are probably familiar with is mental insanity. Duress is another affirmative defense and requires proving, generally, that the only reason the defendant committed the alleged crime was because he or she was under the threat of some danger. I recently had a case where my client was charged with conspiracy to advertise and sell motor vehicles that did not exist. He asserted a duress defense, arguing that the only reason he participated in the conspiracy was because the mob told him that, if he did not do so, he and his family would be murdered. Without direct testimony from my client, it would have been virtually impossible to prove duress. Only the defendant, in this case my client, could explain to the jury why he did what he did, why he acted under duress.

A similar dilemma arises if you are claiming self-defense. Although self-defense is not technically an affirmative defense you have the burden of proving, it can be difficult to prove without your testimony. My client John did not testify in his manslaughter trial, even though he asserted self-defense. But one benefit of being accused of committing a crime in a crowded bar is the presence of a lot of witnesses, at least some of whom could testify that they saw the man John killed attack John first. To the contrary, where a defendant is accused of assaulting a victim in a dark alleyway devoid of witnesses, the defendant may be compelled to testify if he harbors any realistic hopes of convincing a jury that he acted in self-defense.

I can only guarantee one thing when the time comes to make the decision on whether to testify: whatever you choose, if you are found guilty, you will beat up (figuratively, I hope) both yourself and your attorney for a long time. As I write this, past recommendations in trials that resulted in guilty verdicts still haunt me. Before I will even consider recommending to a client that he or she testify, I must be fairly confident that the client is capable of holding up under the pressure of being cross-examined by the prosecutor. Directing a client during direct examination is the easy part. The real challenge is predicting how the client will do when the prosecutor is doing everything in his or her power to make the client look like a liar. Because no matter how much you are prepped by your attorney before the real thing, no matter how hard your attorney tries to simulate cross-examination, grilling you with pointed questions and calling you out on every skeleton in your closet, there is no substitute for the real thing, when you are sitting on the green throne next to the judge, with the peering eyes of twelve jurors watching your every wink, sniffle, and hesitation.

When it comes right down to it, no one knows yourself better than you, and no one knows more about the circumstances surrounding the incident that brought you into the criminal justice system in the first place. This is especially true if you have not told your attorney the whole truth about what happened. Every case is unique, and there is no one all-encompassing golden rule in deciding whether to testify. So, for that reason, the following are what I believe to be the most important considerations to make before making the decision. In providing these considerations, I will assume your trial is before a jury, but they are still relevant even if it is a bench trial.

Do Not Think You Are Going to Convince a Jury You Are Innocent

Everyone thinks that, if they are just given a chance to look someone in the eye and make their case, they can make that person see things their way. I am not sure why this is the case, but it is either overconfidence in one's self or in other human beings. Want proof? Take a look at a politician's approval rating before and after an aired debate. If 1,000 people disliked the politician before the debate, about 1,000 people will dislike that politician after the debate.

Human nature is such that people naturally rush to judge. Every time I select a jury, I always ask whether anyone believes my client is likely guilty simply by virtue of the fact that he has been charged with a crime, and hands always raise. These are people who already presume my client is guilty before even hearing or seeing one piece of evidence. What does this tell you? It tells you that, before you even take the stand to testify on your own behalf, you are likely facing at least a few jurors who already think you are guilty. And this means it is unlikely you will convince those few jurors you are innocent. Those jurors who already think you are guilty will only look for things in you and from you that they can use as further evidence that their initial assumption of guilt was correct. People want to trust their instincts and will protect them even when they fly in the face of logic.

In the play "Hamlet," Queen Gertrude says about someone professing their innocence, "The lady doth protest too much, methinks." What she implies is when a person asserts his or her innocence too aggressively, it can be taken as a sign of dishonesty. How about if your voice shakes because you are nervous? You must be lying. What if you make too much eye contact, or too little? You must be lying. How about if you laugh because you are nervous or shy? You must be lying. And do not laugh at that last one. I once cross-examined a victim who was Asian-American, and every time I asked him a question, he giggled while giving his answer. Now, this was a victim who claimed he was robbed at gunpoint while making a food delivery. The jury later found my client not guilty.

So, after the trial was over, I had the opportunity to speak with the victim and ask him why he laughed when I asked him a serious question. He explained to me that he was just nervous and that laughter or smiling is often a sign of nervousness or shyness in the Asian community. It is just an ingrained social trait. But the jury did not know that. The point is that no matter how hard you try, you will not, by yourself, convince every juror, or sometimes any juror, that you are innocent if you testify. This is especially true given the setting in which you are given the opportunity to convince those jurors. As set forth earlier, direct examination of a witness is governed by strict rules by which questions can be asked and answers given. Taking the stand is not taking the grandstand. It is not an open forum for you to speak directly to the jury and tell them what you think they want to hear. Yes, a capable attorney can ask questions that will allow you to get certain facts to the jury, but it is limited. I am not saying there are not times when testifying is beneficial to you, but never overvalue it.

You Cannot Hide

Unfortunately, when you choose to testify, you give up a certain amount of control over what the judge or jury will hear. It is called opening the door. Opening the door means you are allowing the questioner to elicit certain facts and testimony that would not otherwise be heard by the fact finder if you had not chosen to testify. Some facts may come out through other witnesses regardless of whether you testify. But many things can only come out through you, through the opening you create when you choose to testify.

How far that proverbial door opens depends on several factors. Putting yourself in the witness chair does not give the prosecutor carte blanch to pick and choose any line of questioning or accuse you of anything that comes to mind. There are limitations. For starters, the cross-examination of a witness can generally not exceed the scope of a witness's direct testimony. In other words, when you testify, the prosecutor cannot ordinarily examine you on subjects that were not raised by your attorney during your direct examination. This is why it is important that you only answer the questions posed by your attorney and only offer information that is needed to give an answer.

One of the most common mistakes defendants make is opening the door to a past crime or bad act they have committed. The law limits which, if any, past crimes or bad acts you have committed are allowed to be revealed by the prosecutor to the jury in the event you testify at trial. In fact, before trial begins, upon the request of your attorney, the court will conduct a short hearing involving your attorney and the prosecutor to determine which past crimes and/or bad acts the prosecutor intends to talk about should you testify and which ones, and to what extent, the court will allow. Since the court conducts the hearing before trial begins, you and your attorney will know what things the prosecutor can ask you about if you testify, and the judge's decision on what will be allowed and what will not be allowed is a significant factor in determining whether you should testify.

Past crimes and bad acts you have committed cannot be introduced by the prosecutor for the sole purpose of proving you are more likely to have committed the current charge. For example, the prosecutor in John's bar fight case could not ask John about a previous assault conviction for the sole purpose of convincing the jury he is guilty of assaulting the current victim. Past convictions and bad acts can be raised, however, for the purpose of convincing a judge or jury you are not credible (not being truthful). In determining what to allow, the judge must weigh the likely prejudice the introduction to the jury of any past convictions or bad acts would have on you against its probative value. Judges have a wide discretion in making their decision. Further, it is not an all-or-nothing proposition for the judge. Often, the judge will rule for what is commonly referred to as a Sandoval compromise. Under a Sandoval compromise, the judge allows the prosecutor to reveal to the jury a past conviction but not the details or underlying facts of the conviction. Thus, the prosecutor could ask John if he was previously convicted of assault but could not ask him about the circumstances surrounding the incident and resulting conviction.

The mistake of opening the door to a past crime and/or bad act occurs when you allow the prosecutor to reveal the past crime and/or bad act even after the judge has already precluded the prosecutor from doing so. Here is an example of doing just that thing in a felony DWI trial I recently observed. In that case, the defendant took the stand to testify in his own defense. He was accused of driving while intoxicated by alcohol with his children inside the vehicle. The defendant had been convicted in the past of endangering the welfare of a child. Before trial, the judge had ruled that the prosecutor could not bring up that prior conviction of endangering the welfare of a child.

While on the stand, his attorney asked him if he drove while intoxicated. It was a straightforward question and it called for a straightforward answer: "No." I am sure the defendant's attorney had notified his client that he would ask the question, and I am sure the attorney had fully expected that his client would simply say "No." Well, the defendant did say "No." Unfortunately, he also added, in sum and substance, that he could not have possibly driven while intoxicated because he could never do anything that would put his children in danger. You could sense the exasperation in his attorney, as the door was not just opened but came off its hinges. And the prosecutor wasted no time in walking right on through, asking the defendant if he had not, in fact, been convicted once before of doing the very thing the defendant claimed he could never do: putting his children in danger.

That is an example of opening the door by mistake. But, as mentioned above, you open the door to some extent merely by taking the stand. Hopefully, your attorney will have anticipated the questions that will be asked, and you will be prepared to give the best possible answers. But no matter how much time is spent preparing, there are always questions that either you do not anticipate, or you did anticipate but just do not have a good answer for because the truth is damaging. Further, just because you anticipated a question and have a reasonable answer does not mean it is going to have a positive effect on the jury. Remember, cross-examination allows the questioner to use leading questions. Leading questions do just that: lead. They lead you to responses the questioner wants but you may not. When done properly, cross-examination prevents the witness from merely reciting scripted answers. Control lies with the questioner and not the witness.

Jurors Will Not Hold It Against You if You Do Not Testify

Earlier, I mentioned how there will always be people who see a defendant's failure to testify as a sign of guilt. Most jurors will not. Your right not to testify as a defendant and your right to be presumed innocent are the most stressed rights both before and during the trial process. The right to remain silent throughout trial is a fundamental right in this country. Television shows and movies show suspects being read their Miranda rights, which include the right to remain silent. Prospective jurors (and later jurors) are told and reminded constantly the moment they arrive at the courthouse of the defendant's right not to testify. Your attorney and even most prosecutors remind the jury they cannot hold it against you if you choose not to testify. And through the jury selection process, your attorney gets to ask prospective jurors if they have a problem with you not testifying and disqualify those whom he or she believes do. Jurors have this singular point drilled into them constantly. And having spoken with hundreds of jurors at the conclusion of trials, I have found that my client's decision not to testify was rarely a factor considered by the jurors during their deliberations.

Listen to Your Attorney, But Follow Your Gut

This can be an oxymoron, I know. Sometimes your attorney's advice might run counter to what your gut is telling you. But at the end of the day, you have to trust your attorney's advice regarding whether it is a good idea or not to testify. It is your attorney who will know whether an affirmative defense requires your testimony or whether a jury will likely hold a prior DWI against you if you testify. But at the same time, only you are going to know how you hold up under pressure, whether you stay calm or whether you have a tendency to laugh every time a serious question is posed. My advice is to be honest with your attorney. Share with him or her your concerns, and trust the advice you receive on whether to testify.

Rebuttal Testimony

After both the people and defense rest, the people can seek to re-open their case and present what is called rebuttal testimony. The purpose of rebuttal testimony is to deny evidence that was presented by the defendant. For example, where you present evidence supporting an affirmative defense such as duress, the people can then seek to present witnesses needed to disprove the defense. A witness called by the people for purposes of rebuttal can be a new witness or a witness previously called to testify by the people during their direct case. Offering a witness under the guise of rebuttal for the sole purpose of presenting evidence that could have been presented during the people's direct case is improper. Although, in the interests of justice, the judge has some discretion in allowing such testimony. If the people do present new evidence, your attorney may be given the opportunity to present his or her own rebuttal witness.

Renewed Trial Order of Dismissal/Motion to Dismiss

Earlier in this chapter, I discussed the motion for a trial order of dismissal or motion to dismiss, depending on the jurisdiction. As I explained, this motion is made after the people rest and have no further proof to present. If you present any evidence, the same motion should be made again after you have finished presenting your defense case. Like the first time, the motion is made orally by your attorney on the record outside the presence of the jury. If your attorney is making the motion for the second time, it means the motion was either denied or the judge reserved decision the first time around, and it is highly unlikely the judge will grant the latest motion.

Jury Charge Conference

After all the proof has been presented and your attorney has made his last motion for dismissal, the court will usually next conduct what is called a jury charge conference. The purpose of the jury charge conference is to allow the prosecutor and your attorney a chance to argue for or oppose what will be read to the jury before it begins deliberations, including any lesser included offenses, which are discussed further below. Your attorney should insist that the conference is conducted before closing arguments so he or she can better prepare the closing argument. Without knowing exactly what instructions the jury will receive and what offenses the jury will be asked to consider, it is difficult to effectively prepare.

Typically, the conference is done inside the judge's chambers or at the bench. If it is done in chambers, it is usually done without you, but you have the right to be there if you want. The conference is also usually not done on the record, and the jury is not present. Once the conference is complete, any agreements and/or disputes over the contents of what will be read to the jury are put onto the record, usually inside the courtroom, although again, the jury is not present.

Closing Arguments

After the charge conference but before the jury is read the final instructions, each party has the right to give a closing argument. Most judges will allow the parties at least a lunch break to prepare arguments. However, subject to scheduling issues, including the availability of jurors, and especially in more lengthy trials, most judges will allow the parties to begin closing arguments fresh the next morning. Preparing an effective closing argument requires time to review notes taken during the trial and, when available, transcripts of testimony given during the trial. Whenever possible, your attorney should seek as much time as possible to gather himself or herself and prepare a closing argument.

In most state courts, including those in New York, the defendant's attorney goes first, followed by the prosecutor. In federal court, the prosecutor gives his closing argument, followed by the defendant's attorney. Then, after the defendant's closing argument, the prosecutor is permitted a rebuttal statement. I have always found this extra bite at the apple to be just one more example of how defendants are put at a greater disadvantage in federal criminal trials.

Closing arguments, with the exception of maybe a defense attorney's cross-examination of the people's star witness, is the part of the trial that gets the most attention from the general public. Hollywood loves to portray the closing argument. And famous lawyers like Clarence Darrow and Johnnie Cochran built their reputations on them. Many of you probably remember the famous closing line of Johnnie Cochran during the O.J. Simpson trial: "If the glove doesn't fit, you must acquit."

Closing arguments occur in every jury trial across the country. Almost all of them, unlike the closing arguments of the movies, go unnoticed and uncelebrated. But they are no less important to the defendants in those cases. The closing argument, or summation as it is called sometimes, is your attorney's last chance to speak directly to the jury. It is also your attorney's best chance to speak freely with the jury, as closing arguments generally provide your attorney with more leeway than do opening statements. While the primary purpose of opening statements is to provide the jury with a roadmap of the evidence the attorneys expect the jury to hear and see, the primary purpose of the closing statement is to persuade the jury that the roads on that map go where the attorneys say they go. If you imagine that each piece of evidence is a dot that represents a city on that map, the closing argument seeks to connect those dots.

Like the opening statement, the closing argument is made by your attorney. You cannot speak directly to the jury. Statements made by your attorney during closing arguments are not considered evidence and, as discussed below, the jury will be instructed as much before it begins its deliberations. There are numerous rules governing the content of and the manner in which closing arguments may be made by your attorney, but judges will usually give your attorney wide latitude as long as your attorney avoids giving statements of his or her own personal opinions on the evidence that was presented during the trial and avoids making arguments that are completely unsupported by that evidence.

Every attorney has his or her own style, but all effective closing arguments share certain qualities, including stressing the most favorable facts and suggesting reasonable conclusions and inferences the jury should draw from those facts. Effective closing arguments should also emphasize any inconsistencies and weaknesses in the people's case, including conflicting witness testimony. In doing so, your attorney should constantly remind the jury that you are presumed innocent, and if the jury has any reasonable doubt regarding your guilt, it must find you not guilty. As a personal preference, at either the beginning or end of my closing statements, I like to reintroduce my client and thank all of the jurors on his or her behalf. You should ask your attorney if he or she plans to do so and, if he or she does, you should be prepared to make eye contact with and nod approvingly at the jury at the appropriate moment. Never lose an opportunity to build and reinforce rapport with the jurors. By the end of the trial, you want the jurors to see you as a person and not just a defendant. I will discuss this issue further in the later chapter on courtroom demeanor and presentation.

Charging the Jury

After entertaining all proposals and arguments of counsel, the judge will approve the final instructions, which are then reduced to writing and provided to both the prosecutor and your attorney. After closing arguments are complete, the judge will then read those final instructions, which is called charging the jury.

Aside from the elements of the actual offenses the jury must consider, including any lesser included offenses, most of what is read to the jury is boilerplate instructions and definitions. Most states, including New York, have standard or model instructions. Most judges rely on these standard instructions, in one form or another, exclusively. The standard instructions are only part of the complete instructions. The remainder of the instructions are tailored to fit the particular case.

You should understand what is likely to be read to the jury in your case. Some of the things that will ultimately be read may be difficult to predict because they depend on what happens during the trial, including what witnesses testify and what testimony and evidence is heard and seen by the jury. That said, knowing what a jury will likely hear will give you a better perspective when you have to decide whether to take your case to trial. Below I have provided examples of some of the more common instructions. These are among the instructions I recently used in a recent federal criminal trial. The complete instructions we used were about twice as long:

Function of Judge and Jury

Keep in mind that you, as the jury, are the sole and exclusive judges of the facts. It is your duty to decide each and every issue of fact that has arisen during the course of the trial. No one, not counsel, not the court, may presume to tell you how the issues of fact should be decided. I repeat, that you and you alone are the sole and exclusive judges of the facts.

The credibility, that is, the believability of each witness is itself an issue of fact solely and exclusively within your province as the jury. With respect to each witness, you must determine to what extent you find that witness's testimony credible and acceptable. With respect to any individual witness, you may accept in whole or in part such testimony as you find credible and worthy of belief, and reject in whole or part such testimony as you find unworthy of credit or belief.

As I have stated, you, as the jurors, are the sole and exclusive judges of the facts. On the other hand, I am the sole and exclusive judge of the law. These responsibilities are separate and distinct, and each is of equal importance. As the judge of the law, it has been my function to regulate the course of the trial and to determine what evidence, under the law, was admissible. My rulings in each instance were based solely upon the law. My other function is, of course, to instruct you on the law specifically applicable to this case.

Now, as I say, my instructions to you on the law must be accepted by you whether you agree with them or not. If you have any ideas of your own of what the law is, or what you think it should be, it is now your duty, pursuant to the oath you took as jurors, to disregard your own ideas of the law, and to accept the law exactly as I give it to you. Please remember that all of us, I, as the judge, you as the jury, counsel, and the defendants, are all bound by the laws of our country exactly as those laws provide.

During the course of the trial, I have tried to preside impartially and not express an opinion one way or the other as to what you should find the facts to be. In the course of the trial, it has been necessary for me, from time to time, to rule on the admission of evidence and on motions made with respect to the applicable law. You must not infer from any such ruling I have made, or from anything I have said during the course of the trial, or from these instructions, or from the manner in which they are given, that I hold any views for or against the government or for or against any of the defendants. In that regard, any views of mine would, in any event, not be relevant, since it is your recollection of the evidence and your determination of the issues of fact that controls. With respect to my instructions, you should not single out a particular sentence or any individual point and ignore the rest.

I remind you that each attorney is an officer of the court, owing a high duty to his client. His function is to represent his client to the best of his ability. If, in the interest of advocacy, the attorneys have done or said anything you deem to be objectionable, you must not let such feeling interfere with your primary duty here, which is to judge the facts impartially and to be fair to both the government and the defendant.

At times during the trial, I sustained objections to questions asked without permitting the witness to answer, or where an answer was made, on occasion, instructed that it be stricken from the record and that you disregard. You may not draw any inference from an unanswered question, nor may you consider testimony that has been stricken in reaching your decision. The law requires that your decision be made solely upon the competent evidence before you. Such items as I have excluded from your consideration were excluded because I determined they were not admissible.

Burden of Proof and Presumption of Innocence

Without a doubt, one of the most important safeguards in our law is the presumption of innocence. It simply says all persons charged with a crime and brought to trial are presumed to be innocent unless proven guilty beyond a reasonable doubt. The law, therefore, presumes each of the defendants in this case to be innocent unless proven guilty beyond a reasonable doubt.

Put another way, a defendant is never required to prove anything. On the contrary, the government, having accused a defendant of the crimes charged, has the burden of proving the defendant's guilt beyond a reasonable doubt. The government has the burden of proving the defendant's guilt as to every fact and every element essential to conviction. The burden never shifts. It remains on the government and the presumption of innocence remains with every defendant from the beginning of the trial, until such time, if, during final deliberations, a jury may be convinced that the government has proven a defendant's guilt beyond a reasonable doubt.

Therefore, if in your minds, during your final deliberations, the government has not borne its burden of proof, and the presumption of innocence has not been overcome by proof that convinces you beyond a reasonable doubt, then, of course, you must find the defendant not guilty. On the other hand, if in your minds, during your final deliberations, you are satisfied from all the evidence that the government has borne its burden of proof and that the presumption of innocence has been overcome by evidence that convinces you beyond a reasonable doubt, then you must, of course, find the defendant guilty.

This completes my instructions on the constitutional safeguards of presumption of innocence and the burden of proof. I will now discuss with you the constitutionally mandated standard of proof in all criminal cases, that of proof of guilt beyond a reasonable doubt.

The standard of proof required by law in every criminal case is proof of guilt beyond a reasonable doubt. That standard, however, does not require the government to prove a defendant guilty beyond all possibility of doubt or beyond a shadow of a doubt. It requires the government to establish a defendant's guilt beyond a reasonable doubt. Our law, therefore, requires that before you may convict a defendant, each of you must be satisfied that the credible evidence is sufficient to convince you beyond a reasonable doubt that the defendant is in fact guilty.

The evidence must satisfy you beyond a reasonable doubt that the defendant is, in fact, the person who committed the crime charged. The evidence must also establish beyond a reasonable doubt, each and every essential element of the crime or crimes charged, as I shall later define such elements. What does the law mean when it requires proof of guilt beyond a reasonable doubt? When is a doubt of guilt a reasonable doubt under our law?

A doubt of a defendant's guilt, to be a reasonable doubt, must be based upon reason and common sense. The doubt, to be reasonable, must therefore arise because of the nature and quality of the evidence in the case, or from the lack or insufficiency of the evidence in the case. It is a doubt that would cause a reasonable person to hesitate to act in matter of importance in his or her personal life. Proof beyond a reasonable doubt must, therefore, be proof of such a convincing character that a reasonable person would not hesitate to rely and act upon it in the most important of his or her own affairs.

A doubt of guilt is not reasonable if, instead of being based on the nature and the quality of the evidence or insufficiency of the evidence, it is based upon some guess or whim or speculation unrelated to the evidence in the case. Also, a doubt of guilt is not a reasonable doubt if it is based merely on sympathy for a defendant or from a mere desire by a juror to avoid a disagreeable duty.

I, therefore, repeat that a doubt of a defendant's guilt, to be a reasonable doubt, must arise either from the nature and quality of the evidence in the case, or from the lack or insufficiency of the evidence in the case. If, after fair and impartial consideration of all the evidence in the case, you find that the government has not proven the defendant's guilt beyond a reasonable doubt, as I have defined that term to you, then you must find the defendant not guilty. On the other hand, if you are satisfied that the government has proven the defendant's guilt beyond a reasonable doubt, as I have defined that term to you, then you must find the defendant guilty.

Defendant's Right to Testify

The defendant in this case had a constitutional right not to testify, and if he chose to exercise such right, you may reach no inference of guilt or anything else may be drawn from the fact that he did not testify. For any of you to draw such an inference would be wrong; and indeed, it would be a violation of your oath as a juror.

Credibility of Witnesses

In this case, as in most criminal cases, your decision on the issues of fact which you are required to determine, and on the ultimate issue of fact, the guilt or non-guilt of the defendant, will turn on your estimate of the credibility of each witness's testimony and the weight to be accorded to such testimony.

You, as the jury, must determine the credibility, that is the believability, of each of the witnesses who testified, as well as the proper weight to be accorded to his or her testimony. In simple terms, this means you must decide whether the witness has testified truthfully or whether the witness has testified falsely, or if you are satisfied that the witness has not consciously testified falsely, whether his or her recollection of the events about which he or she has testified is accurate and reliable or inaccurate and unreliable. If it appears that there is a discrepancy in the testimony of the witnesses, you will have to consider whether the apparent discrepancy may be reconciled by fitting the conflicting accounts together. If, however, that is not possible, you will then have to determine which of the conflicting accounts you will accept.

There is no magical formula by which you can evaluate the credibility or believability of a witness. Each of you brings with you into this courtroom all of the experience and background of your everyday lives. In the course of your everyday affairs, you determine for yourselves the reliability or unreliability of things that people tell you. The same tests you use in your everyday dealings are the tests you will apply in your deliberations. In this regard, I will now explain a few tests you should use.

Is the witness an interested or disinterested witness? If he or she is interested in the outcome of the trial on one side or the other, you should consider such interest in determining how much credit or weight you will give to his or her testimony. A witness is an interested witness when by reason of relationship, friendship, antagonism, or prejudice in favor of or against one side or the other, his or her testimony, in your judgment, is biased, or likely to be biased, toward the side he or she favors.

Another test you should consider is the test of consistency. To determine whether testimony is worthy of belief, it should be weighed with and against the testimony of other witnesses with equal opportunity to observe and recall the same events. Is the testimony consistent or inconsistent with other testimony in this case?

Moreover, to determine whether you believe a specific witness, you should consider whether his or her testimony at the trial is inconsistent with any prior statement he or she made. If you find that any prior statement made by a witness was not consistent with his testimony at trial, you should decide whether that affects the believability of the witness's testimony at this trial. Additionally, where the prior statement was made under oath you can consider it not only for the purpose of judging the credibility of the witness, but also for its truth.

Another test: In determining the credibility of any witness, you should consider his or her demeanor and manner of testifying on the stand. Did the witness strike you as being frank, open, and certain or evasive, deceptive, and unsure? Did the witness's memory of the events concerning which he or she testified, appear to you to be accurate or hazy? Did the witness have an opportunity to really see, hear, and know the events concerning which he or she testified?

In determining the credibility of a witness, you should consider whether such witness has any bias or prejudice for or against any party in the case. In determining the credibility and weight to be given to the testimony of a witness, you should take into account such bias or prejudice.

If you find that any witness has knowingly, that is, willfully and intentionally, testified falsely as to any material fact, that is, as to an important matter, you have the right to conclude that the witness also lied about other matters. You are not required, however, to consider such a witness as totally unworthy of belief. You may accept so much of the witness's testimony as you deem to be true and disregard what you feel is false. As to the witnesses who testified, even if you find that the testimony given by any witness was not contradicted by any other evidence in the case, such finding does not relieve you of your duty and responsibility to evaluate the credibility of the witness and to make your own determination of what weight, if any, you will give such testimony.

Testimony of Law Enforcement

You will recall that several law enforcement officers testified in this case. You should use the same tests in evaluating their testimony as you use in evaluating the testimony of any other witness. In other words, the mere fact that a witness is a law enforcement officer does not require that his or her testimony be given any greater or lesser credibility than that of any other witness. In that regard, it is certainly permissible for counsel to question the credibility of a law enforcement officer as with any other witness.

Direct and Circumstantial Evidence

As to evidence, there are two kinds: direct and circumstantial. Direct evidence is proof of a fact, such as testimony of an eyewitness that the witness saw something. Circumstantial evidence is indirect evidence that is proof of a fact or facts from which you could draw the inference, by reason and common sense, that another fact exists, even though it has not been proven directly. Of course, this process of drawing inferences from facts in evidence is not a matter of guesswork or speculation. You are entitled to consider both kinds of evidence. The law permits you to give equal weight to both, but it is for you to decide how much weight to give to any evidence.

Arguments and Statements of Attorneys

Arguments and statements by the lawyers are not evidence. The lawyers were not witnesses in this case. What they may have said in their closing arguments, just like what they said in opening statements, and at other times during the trial, was intended to help you interpret the evidence, but it is not evidence. If the facts as you remember them differ from the way the lawyers have stated them, your memory of the facts controls.

Further, questions and objections by the lawyers are not evidence. Attorneys have a duty to object when they believe a question is improper under the rules of evidence. You should not be influenced by the objection or by the way I ruled on it.

Indictment Not Evidence

The indictment is not evidence. It is only an accusation required by the law, solely for the purpose of informing a defendant of the offenses with which he or she is charged. It is simply a paper writing. It is not, I repeat not, evidence of anything. The allegations set forth in the indictment are allegations only. They are not evidence. As I say, the indictment is merely a device required by law to inform a defendant of the charges against him or her and to bring such charges to trial. The indictment proves nothing.

Sympathy

Members of the jury, please remember at all times that you are not advocates for one side or the other. You are judges, judges of the facts. Your sole interest is to seek the truth from the evidence in this case. In reaching your verdict, you may not consider or speculate concerning matters relating to sentence or punishment. If you return a verdict of guilty, sentence or punishment is a matter for the judge alone. Therefore, I emphasize that you are not to consider, nor are you to discuss any matters relating to sentence or punishment.

Likewise, in reaching your verdict, you are not to be affected by sympathy, bias, or prejudice. In that regard, you must not let any personal feelings concerning race, national origin, or age influence your verdict. Nor, must you let any personal feelings concerning the nature of the crimes charged interfere with your decision-making process. Further, you must not be influenced by what you might believe the reaction to your verdict will be, whether it will please or displease anyone, be popular or unpopular, or indeed, any consideration outside the case as it has been presented to you in this courtroom. You should consider only the evidence (both the testimony and exhibits), find the facts from what you consider to be the believable evidence, apply the law as I have given it to you, to those facts. Your verdict will be determined by the conclusions thus reached.

Also, keep in mind that your function to reach a decision based on the evidence and the law is a very important one. When you are in the jury room, listen to each other, and discuss the evidence and issues in the case among yourselves. It is the duty of each of you, as jurors, to consult with one another, and to deliberate with a view toward reaching agreement on a verdict, if you can do so without violating your individual judgment and your conscience. While you should not surrender honest convictions of what the truth is and of the weight and effect of the evidence, and while each of you must decide the case yourself and not merely consent to the decision of other members of the jury, you should examine the issues and the evidence before you with candor and frankness, and with proper respect and regard for the opinions of each other.

Members of the jury, this case is obviously important to both the government and to the defendant. Therefore, they and I rely upon you to give full and conscientious attention and consideration to the issues in evidence before you. By doing so, you will carry out to the fullest your oaths as jurors to truly try the issues of this case and render a true verdict.

Deliberation

The final phase of any jury trial is the jury's deliberation. Deliberation is when the jury retreats to the jury room to decide whether you are guilty or not guilty. What exactly goes on inside the jury room is a mystery to even many seasoned attorneys. I have overheard more than a few attorneys speak about the amount they would give up to be a fly on the wall inside a jury room during a deliberation. I would be dishonest if I claimed I know. Fortunately, I have taken the opportunity to speak with numerous juries post-verdict, and from those conversations, I have at least learned a little about what normally goes on.

The typical jury usually starts the deliberation by taking an informal vote to get an idea of what everyone is thinking. That initial vote rarely results in twelve votes one way or the other. But occasionally, when everyone is in agreement, and no one feels there is a chance their mind will change, the jury comes back with a verdict. When you hear stories of how a jury was out only five minutes before returning its verdict, that is how it usually happens.

What happens more often is the initial vote reveals that there is some split among those who believe the defendant is guilty and those who believe the defendant is not guilty or, at minimum, there are jurors who acknowledge their vote could be swayed. When this occurs, the thing that normally happens next is the jurors walk each other through the evidence, and in one form or another, debate each other's respective positions. Normally, it is the foreman who referees the process from inside the jury room. The foreman is the juror who acts as the mouthpiece of the jury. When notes need to be written, the foreman writes them. The foreman reads the verdict, and the foreman speaks directly to the judge when it is needed. That said, it is not always the foreman who dictates the flow of the deliberation process. The jury room is a microcosm of the real world, where stronger personalities tend to lead and the meek follow. In most courts, the foreman is chosen randomly, often the first juror who is selected. Thus, there is no guarantee that the foreman will equate to taking charge inside the jury room.

Deliberation follows the reading of the jury charge. Depending on the time of day, the judge's schedule, and the known availability of the jurors, deliberation may begin immediately, or it may begin the next day. If it is late in the day, the judge may elect to allow the jury to start fresh in the morning. Except in rare cases, juries are no longer sequestered in most states, including New York. That is, they do not spend the night together at a hotel. Instead, they are allowed to return to their own homes, with the warning from the judge not to speak about the trial to anyone, including each other. If there is a reasonable amount of time for the jury to reach a verdict, most defendants usually prefer that deliberations begin immediately. After all, by this time, you have probably already spent more than a few sleepless nights, and why spend one more if it is not necessary. But at the same, depending on the verdict, it could be the last night you spend in your own bed.

You also want the jury to reach a verdict that is not affected by the pressures of time or sheer exhaustion. This is especially true if you think the jurors leaning towards a not-guilty verdict are in the minority. You want those jurors on your side to stick to their guns. If they think persuading the majority to change their positions is futile, they may feel it is pointless to come back tomorrow. This could, of course, work in your favor if you believe you have the majority leaning towards a not-guilty verdict. In the end, it is simply impossible to know whether it is to your advantage or disadvantage starting deliberations near the end of the day. For that reason, if there exists a realistic chance that a verdict can be reached the day deliberation begins, I generally prefer deliberation begins as soon as possible.

Whenever they begin, before the jury enters the jury room, in addition to reading the jury instructions, the judge will also set some ground rules for handling questions and reviewing any exhibits that were entered into evidence during the course of the trial. Exhibits are pieces of evidence that were presented and admitted into evidence by the judge during the trial. They include any documents and property that was seized during law enforcement's investigation. In a typical drug possession case, the drugs are usually an exhibit. In a murder case or gun possession case where a weapon was found, the weapon is usually an exhibit.

Exhibits are not typically given to the jury when they enter the jury room to begin deliberations. Instead, the jury is given a list of all of the exhibits and is asked to make a request if it wants to see a particular exhibit. A request is usually made by the foreman writing a note and passing it to the courtroom deputy that is assigned to guard the jury room. Before the jury begins deliberations, the judge will also ask the attorneys if it is acceptable to provide the jury an exhibit upon request. The alternative is to have the attorneys return to the courtroom every time the jury requests an exhibit. For obvious reasons, certain exhibits, such as drugs and weapons, will not be given to the jury outside the attorneys' supervision.

As stated previously, the jury is also not provided with the written transcript of all the testimony that was presented during the trial. If the jury wants to have a witness's testimony read back, or has a question on the law or any other aspect of the court's charge, the jury must make a request to the court the same way it would request an exhibit. In the event such a request is made, everyone, including you, must be present. Say, for example, the jury wants to hear the testimony of the victim. The foreman will prepare and pass a note requesting the testimony, hopefully specifying whether it wishes for all the testimony or just a portion of the testimony read back. The jury can choose to have the testimony read in its entirety. It could ask for just the direct examination or cross-examination testimony, or it could just ask for testimony given in response to specific questions.

After receiving the request, the deputy will then inform the court, and the court will then contact your attorney and the prosecutor requesting them to return to the courtroom with you. Before a read-back can be given, the court has to determine exactly what the jury is seeking so the stenographer can locate the testimony. This is not as simple as it may sound. Often, jury notes are poorly written, difficult to read, and/or fail to contain enough specificity regarding exactly what it wants read. If the court cannot deduce exactly what it wants, the jury can be brought back into the courtroom to clarify its request. This issue can sometimes become a bone of contention between your attorney and the prosecutor, as each side prefers that only favorable testimony be read back.

If it is a question on the law or another part of the jury charge, the judge will first attempt to come to an agreement with your attorney and the prosecutor on how to best answer the question. Again, this is sometimes not as easy as it may sound. Often, the jury's question is confusing. If there exists any confusion over the question, the judge will usually advise the jury of the nature of the confusion and request that the jury submit a new question or clarify in writing the original one.

There is no time in a trial that causes more anxiety than the deliberation process. Deliberations can last five minutes or they can last days. For your attorney, every time his or her phone rings, it could be the court asking him or her to return to the courtroom for a verdict. For you, every time you receive a telephone call or a visit from your attorney, you could find out that there is a verdict. Perhaps the most aggravating part of the process is the jury's requests for read-backs or to have questions answered. Usually, when the court asks the parties to return to the courtroom, the court does not advise the parties regarding the purpose of the return trip, in which case you will not know until you get back to the courtroom whether the jury has reached a verdict or merely has a question. Sometimes the court clerk will give a nod one way or the other to your attorney. This is another time it helps to have an attorney who has a good relationship with the court's staff.

The Verdict

Whether it takes five minutes or five days, there are two conclusions to the deliberation process: a verdict or a hung jury, which results in a mistrial. A hung jury is when the jury advises the court that it cannot reach a unanimous decision regarding guilt or innocence on at least one count of the indictment. Remember that whatever verdict the jury reaches, it must be unanimous. That means, on a twelve-juror trial, all twelve jurors must either find you guilty or not guilty on every charge the jury has been asked to consider. The court will do everything in its power to avoid a hung jury, including ordering the jury to keep trying to reach a unanimous verdict. The court will also usually ask your attorney and the prosecutor whether the jury should be given more time to reach a verdict. Deciding whether to argue for or against is a tricky call. Obviously, if you feel the majority of the jurors wish to vote not guilty, you would rather the court lean on the jury as much as possible to return a verdict.

Hung juries are rare, but there are cases in which the jury is simply too divided to reach a unanimous verdict. I am actually surprised that it does not happen more often than it does, given it only takes one juror with a contrary view of the evidence to be committed to his or her opinion to such a degree that he or she will not be swayed by the other jurors. If the judge determines that no amount of additional time will resolve the division, the judge must declare a hung jury and order a mistrial.

A mistrial does not mean you have won the war. It is debatable whether it even constitutes winning the battle. Mistrials leave the prosecutor with the option of trying the case again, and you are not protected by the principle of double jeopardy. In the event of a mistrial, if the prosecutor chooses to retry the case, a new trial does not occur immediately, and it is not conducted before the same jury. If you are in custody at the time of the trial, you could have to remain there until the second trial goes forward. If the prosecutor decides to try it again, the people notify you and your attorney of their intention, and the court schedules a new trial, usually months into the future, depending on the schedules of the court, prosecutor, and your attorney.

A hung jury and resulting mistrial is certainly a better result than a guilty verdict. The prosecutor does not always choose to retry the case. And having a second chance to defend the case at trial can have its advantages. But it can also have its disadvantages. Things that went wrong for the prosecutor can be fixed or avoided the second time around. Strategic decisions made by you and your attorney that might have caught the prosecutor off guard during the first trial are less likely to do so the second time.

When the final call or word from the court comes, you and your attorney may not know it. Again, unless your attorney gets a nod, you may not know it is a verdict until the judge announces that a verdict has been reached. Often the nod comes from one of the court's deputies. They are the ones that remain in the courtroom outside the jury room during deliberations. They are usually the first to know when a verdict is reached and what that verdict is. During my last jury trial, one of the courtroom deputies who I have known for years pulled me aside before we entered the courtroom and whispered into my ear that my client will be pleased with the verdict. He asked that I not let my client know and, of course, I let my client know, as discreetly as possible. If your attorney is not given any advanced warning, one of the surest ways of knowing a verdict has been reached when you enter the courtroom is if you notice extra security inside and around the courtroom. Most courthouses have policies that require additional deputies to be present inside the courtroom when verdicts are read, to ensure the safety of the jury, prosecutor, and court personnel. Do not be alarmed. It does not mean the verdict is guilty. The additional help arrives regardless of the verdict.

Once you are reasonably sure a verdict is forthcoming, you should take a minute to compose yourself and say last goodbyes to any family and friends who are present. If the verdict is guilty, the judge could remand you into custody immediately to await sentencing. You should be aware of this possibility so you are as prepared as possible to leave everyone and everything behind. Obviously, if you are already in custody at the time of trial, you do not need to be concerned with these issues.

If you are not in custody, you should also do what you can to compose your family and friends and prepare them for the possible outcome of a guilty verdict. The process of preparation should have already begun, but in the pressures of the moment, it never hurts to remind everyone one last time. With the heavy burden resting on your shoulders, it is easy to forget that you have loved ones who are just as frightened by the prospect of losing you. I try to explain to both my client and my client's family and friends that, if the jury returns a guilty verdict, there will be a wave of shock that envelopes them. I ask them to avoid any outbursts that could upset the judge. You need to remember that, even if the verdict comes back guilty, the case is not over. You will still need to be sentenced, which lies within the judge's discretion. You may also file certain post-conviction motions that are decided by the judge. Getting outwardly angry or disrespectful serves no purpose other than to possibly prejudice you.

When you enter the courtroom, the jury will not be there. The same as it is any other time you may have been summoned back to the courtroom for read-backs or questions, the judge will read the jury's note onto the record, this time, however, announcing that the jury has reached a verdict. The judge will them ask the parties whether they are ready for the jury to re-enter the courtroom, and the jury will be let back in from the jury room. After entering the courtroom, the judge may or may not ask you and your attorney to stand for the reading of the verdict. The judge will then ask the foreman if, in fact, the jury has reached a verdict, and the foreman will answer either "Yes" or "No." Assuming the answer is "Yes," the judge will then state, in sum and substance, "With respect to count I of the indictment charging the defendant with [crime], how does the jury find the defendant, guilty or not guilty?" After the foreman gives the answer, the judge will repeat the question for every crime included in the jury charge until the jury has given its verdict with respect to every such charge.

Polling the Jury

After the verdict is read, the judge will ask if either your attorney or the prosecutor wants the jury polled. Polling a jury is when the court clerk asks each individual juror to state affirmatively that he or she agrees with the verdict. It ensures that the verdict is, in fact, unanimous by forcing each individual juror to announce that he or she voted the same as every other juror. While it may seem pointless, your attorney has nothing to lose by polling the jury if the jury returns a guilty verdict. The purpose of polling is to put each juror on the spot, to force each juror to stand under the spotlight and tell the judge that he or she found the defendant guilty beyond a reasonable doubt and did not just acquiesce to the will of the other jurors. Most importantly, it is your last hope of a not-guilty verdict. While exceptionally rare, jurors have been known to change their vote during polling. Thus, if you find yourself on the wrong end of the verdict, you should insist that your attorney request the jury be polled.

Not Guilty

The verdict must be either guilty or not guilty with respect to each charge. The following chapter discusses the ramifications of the guilty verdict. If the verdict is not guilty, you are immediately relieved of all obligations to the court. If you are not in custody, you are free to walk out of the courtroom, never to look back. If you are out on bail, your attorney should ask that the court order that any cash that was posted as bail be released to the person who posted it. He or she should also request that any personal property being held by the prosecutor or law enforcement be released to you.

If you are in custody, you must be immediately released. "Immediately" does not mean you walk straight out of the courtroom. Ordinarily, you must still be taken back to the facility in which you are being held to be processed before being released for good. Processing may take a couple of hours.

6

What Happens if I Am Found Guilty?

"There is no man so good, who, were he to submit all his thoughts and action to the laws, would not deserve hanging ten times in his life."
—Michel De Montaigne, sixteenth-century French writer

Your heart is already throbbing to get outside your chest when you hear the word no defendant wishes to hear: "guilty." But after the jury has been polled, it is time to move forward. You must move forward. Moving forward means facing both short-term consequences and longer-term ones.

The most immediate concern is your custody status. If you are already in custody, you will remain in custody. Handcuffs will be immediately put back on, and you will be ushered out of the courtroom and back to jail. If you are not already in custody, you could be taken into custody to await sentencing. It is up to the judge's discretion whether to allow you to remain free under your current release conditions, if any, or to take you into custody.

You should be prepared to be taken into custody, which means giving any personal possessions, such as your wallet, purse, and mobile phone, to someone you trust or your attorney to hold onto. Your attorney should have a pretty good idea before the time comes whether the judge will take you into custody. Knowing your judge is important. Some judges are more likely to take defendants into custody than others. The seriousness of the crime, including the length of your possible sentence, is also an important factor. Generally speaking, the more time you face, the more likely it is that the judge will take you into custody. Judges have to take into account the likelihood that, if released, you will skip town and fail to return for sentencing. In a judge's eyes, if you are facing life in prison, you are more likely to drive across the border to Mexico or Canada than the defendant facing eight months in the local jail.

You are also less likely to be taken into custody if you have already posted some bail. Whether it is cash or bond, the judge is not likely to revoke it if it has already been posted. The judge could choose to increase the amount of the bail, but that is rare.

If you are convicted following trial, you must be sentenced. Sentencing is the job of the judge. The jury has no say in sentencing. It is unlikely you will be sentenced immediately. Sentencing is normally scheduled for another date and time. If the possible sentence includes jail time, sentencing will likely be set weeks, or even months, into the future. If a pre-sentence investigation report is ordered, sentencing could take as long as three months, depending on how long it will take the department of probation to complete the report. The longer you have to prepare for sentencing, the better. Just as it is important to prepare diligently for trial, it is just as important to prepare appropriately for sentencing.

Pre-Sentence Investigation Report

In New York, a pre-sentence investigation report must be prepared any time a defendant can serve at least six months in jail or prison. In New York, the pre-sentence investigation report is prepared by the Department of Probation for the county where your trial was held. The purpose of the report is to provide the sentencing judge with relevant information needed to render a fair sentence. It is intended as a tool to assist the judge. The report will include your criminal history, family information, employment information, any history of drug and/or alcohol abuse, and any other information the probation officer believes is relevant. A typical report also summarizes your strengths and weaknesses as they relate to demonstrating lawful behavior in the future, the probation officer's opinion regarding your chances of re-offending, and the probation officer's sentence recommendation.

Before preparing their report, a probation officer will interview you. The interview is usually conducted at the probation officer's office, and it takes about an hour from soup to nuts. The personal interview is very important, as what you have to say will be included in the report and will weigh heavily on the officer's ultimate recommendation. You should treat it like you would a job interview. Dress appropriately. If you are a man, wear a suit or at least a shirt and tie. If you are a woman, wear a business suit or a conservative dress. Be courteous and respectful. Do not take out any residual animosity you have over the conviction on the probation officer. Remember, the probation officer is only doing his or her job. He or she had nothing to do with the decision to prosecute you, and he or she has no personal interest in seeing the judge sentence you harshly.

You have a right to have your attorney present during the interview, and I highly recommend that you insist upon your attorney's presence. If you remember nothing else, remember this: Do not attempt to explain to the probation officer why you are not guilty, how you were unjustly convicted, or otherwise attempt to skirt or shift the blame. This applies even if you really were unjustly convicted or are not guilty. If you have ever seen the movie "Shawshank Redemption," you might remember the part where a new inmate asks Tim Robbins's character what he is in for, and Robbins's character replies, "Me? My lawyer f***ed me. Everybody's innocent in here. Didn't you know that?" It was a light moment in the movie and poked fun at the truth that almost every convict swears innocence to the very end. Probation officers know this. Judges know this.

If you try explaining why you are really not guilty, the probation officer, no matter how compelling you are and no matter whether you really are innocent, will not believe you. And I can almost promise you that somewhere in his or her report, he or she will remark on how you are still failing to take responsibility for your actions, and the judge who sentences you will conclude that you need a harsher sentence. You see, judges, in deciding an appropriate sentence, have three primary aims: (1) rehabilitation, (2) penalization, and (3) deterrence. In other words, they want to render a sentence that will punish you, deter you from violating the law again, and treat the personal shortcomings that led you to violate the law in the first place. Taking responsibility for your unlawful actions, whether genuine or not, demonstrates to the judge and, possibly later down the road, to the parole board, that you have began the rehabilitation process, have taken your punishment seriously, and are unlikely to violate the law again. Therefore, I cannot stress enough the importance of not pleading innocence during the interview.

You will be asked at some point during the interview whether you wish to discuss the incident that led to your arrest and ultimate conviction. I recommend one of two things. Either you admit wrongdoing and show remorse, or you explain that, at your attorney's advice, you do not wish to discuss the incident but regret what happened. Either way, you are not expressly denying wrongdoing and you are always showing remorse. If your attorney is present during the interview, as I recommend, he or she can tell the probation officer that you have been advised not to discuss the incident. Regardless, the importance of expressing remorse, whether specifically regarding what it is alleged that you did or just in general, cannot be overstated.

Before you are sentenced, you should review the report. Ideally, the report is provided to your attorney, and your attorney will have the opportunity to review it with you before you arrive in court for sentencing. In practice, however, it is not uncommon for your attorney to receive the report when he or she walks in the courtroom for sentencing. Either way, you have the right to, and should, review the report closely to ensure its contents are accurate. Often, the report's author mishears statements you make during the interview or includes inaccurate information. It is important that the information is accurate. Not only will the judge use the report to sentence you, but if you have to go before a parole board for possible early or conditional release from prison, the parole board will use it. It can also be used should you ever be convicted again of another crime or if you violate the terms of your probation or parole after you are released from prison. So, whenever you receive the report, be sure to review it closely with your attorney. If you locate any inaccuracies, your attorney should advise the judge and make the appropriate objections in court.

Character Letters

The pre-sentence investigation report is only one thing the judge reviews before handing down a sentence. Your attorney may also submit his or her own written statement for the judge's consideration. In federal court, before sentencing, your attorney prepares and files with the court a pre-sentence memorandum. A pre-sentence memorandum or statement sets forth the reasons the judge should render a lenient sentence. It should focus on your best qualities, things like your marital status, children for whom you bear responsibility, employment status, charitable endeavors, to name just a few.

I also encourage you to submit letters from people who can vouch for your character and reputation (assuming, of course, they say good things about you). You should attempt to procure letters from a wide range of people in your life, not just letters from friends and family members. The most helpful letters come from individuals who are less likely to be biased in your favor (i.e., letters from non-family members and friends). Potential sources include co-workers, employers, priests or pastors, ex-wives/husbands or ex-boyfriends/girlfriends, your doctor, law enforcement officials, your children, the list is endless. The more the better. The wider the sample range the better. You will note I listed your ex-significant others as a potential source. If you have maintained a positive relationship, this can be the most persuasive reference of the bunch. This is someone whose opinion the sentencing judge will take seriously, as he or she has every reason in the world not to write positively about you.

Get these letters well in advance of your sentencing date. The sooner the judge receives them, the more likely it is the judge will actually read them and consider them in deciding an appropriate sentence. The letters should go to the court through your attorney, either from you or directly from the letter's author. Some people may feel more comfortable sending the letter to your attorney, since the letter is about you. If the letters are sent directly to the court, the judge may not review them. Additionally, you want your attorney to read them first to make sure they are appropriate. The last thing you want is that ex-girlfriend taking this opportunity to shovel some dirt onto your casket.

You should never write a letter for someone, and you should not dictate what the person includes in the letter, as it could have the opposite effect of discouraging the person from writing nice things about you. It is okay to give the person some general guidelines and ideas of what to include in the letter. Over the years, I have received and read countless letters. The following is a simple but effective letter (with some minor modifications to conceal names):

> Dear Judge Ham:
>
> My name is Bert Eggs. I am a peer counselor at the YMCA in Rochester, New York. For the past four years, Ann Green has worked as a volunteer at the YMCA under my direct supervision, working with youth of various ages. During this time period, Ms. Green worked approximately ten hours per week. While she was not compensated for her work, she always appeared when scheduled and always arrived to work on time.
>
> Over the past years, I have had the privilege to get to know Ms. Green on both a personal and professional basis. Ms. Green is not only a hard worker but a caring and loyal friend. She is always the first one to offer a lending hand when someone is in need. It is a privilege to work beside her and to call her a friend.
>
> Sincerely,
> Bert Eggs

Statement with Respect to Sentencing Factors

If you are convicted in federal court, your attorney should file a document called a statement with respect to sentencing factors prior to sentencing. The purpose of the document is to set forth any objections you may have to the pre-sentence report and to set forth what factors you believe the judge should consider in formulating an appropriate sentence. This is especially important in federal court because of the Advisory Guidelines, which are established guidelines intended to be used by the judge as an advisory tool in formulating the appropriate sentence.

The Advisory Guidelines result in a recommended sentencing range. The recommended sentencing range to be used in your case is calculated using a formula comprised of two components: an offense level score and a criminal history category. Once the offense level score and criminal history category number are determined, a chart dictates the applicable sentencing range. Determining the correct offense level score and criminal history category is complicated, which is why few criminal defense attorneys practice in both state and federal court; federal court practice is a very specialized area of law. You will need to trust that your attorney has the knowledge and experience necessary to ensure the correct sentencing range is determined.

It is important to remember that the recommended sentencing range is only that: a recommendation. It is only one factor to be used by the federal judge in sentencing you. The statement with respect to sentencing factors should set forth not only the recommended sentencing range but all other positive factors that are relevant in your case. The following is a streamlined example of a statement with respect to sentencing factors I filed in a case wherein my client was convicted following a jury trial:

IN THE UNITED STATES DISTRICT COURT
FOR THE WESTERN DISTRICT OF NEW YORK

UNITED STATES OF AMERICA,
Plaintiff,

-vs-

JOHN DOE,
Defendant.

DEFENDANT'S STATEMENT WITH RESPECT TO SENTENCING FACTORS

The Defendant, JOHN DOE, through undersigned counsel, states as follows:

1. Defendant hereby submits this statement pursuant to Local Procedural Guidelines under the Sentencing Reform Act of 1984.
2. The undersigned hereby certifies that he has received a copy of the pre-sentence report (PSR) and represents that the defendant has one objection to the factual determinations made in the PSR.

3. The Defendant has no objections to the PSR.

OFFENSE LEVEL COMPUTATIONS

4. Defendant agrees that, pursuant to the Advisory Guidelines, Defendant's criminal history category is level I and total offense level is 24.
5. Defendant agrees that, based on those calculations, his sentencing range under the Advisory Guidelines is 51 to 63 months.

FACTORS EFFECTING SENTENCE

6. As this Court is aware, in *United States v. Booker*, 125 S. Ct. 738 (2005),[1] the Supreme Court held that the mandatory guideline system created by the Sentencing Reform Act of 1984 (SRA) was unconstitutional. Therefore, the appropriate remedial measure was to declare the Guidelines merely advisory. *See Booker*, 125 S. Ct. at 757 (2005) (Breyer, J.). After *Booker*, federal sentencing is vastly different. Treating the Guidelines as advisory requires that the Court consider the guideline range calculation as merely one of many factors in determining a sentence no greater than necessary to achieve the goals of sentencing set forth in 18 U.S.C. §3553(a)(2).[2]

A. The §3553(a) Sentencing Mandate

7. Section 3553(a) is comprised of two distinct parts: the so-called "sentencing mandate" contained in the prefatory clause of §3553(a) and the "factors" to be considered in fulfilling that mandate. The overriding mandate of §3553(a)[3] requires district courts to impose a sentence "sufficient, but not greater than necessary," to comply with the four purposes of sentencing set forth in §3553(a)(2): (a) retribution, (b) deterrence, (c) incapacitation, and (d) rehabilitation. *United States v. Pullen*, 89 F.3d 368 (7th Cir. 1996).[4]

---

[1] *U.S. v. Booker*, 543 U.S. 220, 125 S. Ct. 738, 160 L. Ed. 2d 621 (2005).
[2] 18 U.S.C.A. §3553(a)(2).
[3] 18 U.S.C.A. §3553(a).
[4] *U.S. v. Pullen*, 89 F.3d 368 (7th Cir. 1996).

8. The sufficient-but-not-greater-than-necessary requirement is often referred to as the "parsimony provision." The parsimony provision is not just another "factor" to be considered along with the others set forth in §3553(a). Instead, it sets an independent limit on the sentence a court may impose. *See United States v. Siegel*, 217 Fed. Appx. 115 (2d Cir. 2008).[5] Since §3553(a) requires sentence to be no greater than necessary to meet four purposes of sentencing, imposition of sentence greater than necessary to meet those purposes is reversible, even if within Guideline range. *Id.*
9. In determining the sentence minimally sufficient to comply with the §3553(a)(2) purposes of sentencing, the court must consider several factors listed in §3553(a). These factors include:

> (1) the nature and circumstances of the offense and the history and characteristics of the defendant; (2) the need to reflect the seriousness of the offense, to promote respect for the law, and to provide just punishment for the offense; (3) the need for deterrence; (4) the need to protect the public; (5) the need to provide the defendant with needed educational or vocational training or medical care; (6) the kinds of sentences available; (7) the sentencing guidelines range; (8) pertinent policy statements of the Sentencing Commission; (9) the need to avoid unwanted sentencing disparities; and (10) the need to provide restitution to victims.

United States v. Capanelli, 479 F.3d 163, 165 (2d Cir. 2007).[6]

10. While district courts must in all cases "consider" the Guideline range, *United States v. Booker*, 543 U.S. 220, 245-46 (2005),[7] the Guidelines do not subordinate the other factors in §3553(a). Rather, it is the parsimony provision that serves as "the guidepost for

---

[5] *U.S. v. Siegel*, 271 Fed. Appx. 115 (2d Cir. 2008).
[6] *U.S. v. Capanelli*, 479 F.3d 163, 165 (2d Cir. 2007).
[7] *U.S. v. Booker*, 543 U.S. 220, 245-46, 125 S. Ct. 738, 160 L. Ed. 2d 621 (2005).

sentencing decisions post-*Booker*." *United States v. Ferguson*, 456 F.3d 660, 667 (6th Cir. 2006).[8]

11. Sentencing courts have a duty to consider many factors the Guidelines specifically exclude from consideration (even factors prohibited by the formerly mandatory Guidelines) in determining the type of sentence that satisfies the sentencing mandate of §3553(a). *See United States v. Winingear*, 422 F.3d 1211, 1246 (11th Cir. 2005)[9] (declining to address whether sentences within the Guidelines range were per se reasonable, holding that as long as the sentence complied with 18 U.S.C. §3553(a),[10] the sentence was reasonable).
12. The sentencing judge, after considering §3553(a) and §3661 factors (including the Guidelines), has full discretion to sentence anywhere within the statutory range. If the *Booker* court thought otherwise—if it thought the Guidelines not only had to be "considered" (as the amputated statute requires) but had generally to be followed—its opinion would surely say so. *Booker*, 125 S. Ct. at 791 (Scalia, J., dissenting). Likewise, if the remedial majority thought the Guidelines had to be given "heavy weight," its opinion would have said so. The remedial majority clearly understood that giving any special weight to the Guidelines range relative to the other factors would violate the Sixth Amendment. "A sentence may be unreasonable if it is the product of a procedure that does not follow *Booker*'s requirements, regardless of the actual sentence. After a district court has accurately calculated the *Guidelines* range, it may impose a more severe or more lenient sentence as long as the final sentence is reasonable. *United States v. Singletary*, 458 F.3d 72 (2d Cir. 2006).[11]

B. *Mitigating Factors To Be Considered in Determining a Reasonable Sentence Under 18 U.S.C. §3553(a)(2).*

13. As set forth above, after *Booker*, this court is statutorily required to impose a sentence that is minimally sufficient to accomplish the

---

[8] *U.S. v. Ferguson*, 456 F.3d 660, 667, 2006 FED App. 0286P (6th Cir. 2006).
[9] *U.S. v. Winingear*, 422 F.3d 1241, 1246 (11th Cir. 2005).
[10] 18 U.S.C.A. §3553(a).
[11] *U.S. v. Singletary*, 458 F.3d 72 (2d Cir. 2006).

purposes of sentencing, and the Guidelines are only one of five equally important factors to be considered in determining the minimally sufficient sentence. In the instant case, a sentence at the statutory minimum is sufficient to satisfy the goals of (1) retribution, (2) deterrence, (3) incapacitation, and (4) rehabilitation. Imposition of sentence greater than necessary to meet those purposes is reversible, even if such a sentence falls within the Guidelines range.

1. <u>The Defendant's Remorse, Contrition, Desire for Rehabilitation, and Age</u>

14. Remorse is a factor the Court must consider in sentencing a defendant. *United States v. Fagan*, 162 F.3d 1280, 1284-85 (10th Cir. 1998).[12] Under the old departure analysis, "Because remorse is not a prohibited factor, but a factor already considered in the Sentencing Guidelines, a sentencing court may depart downward if it finds that remorse is present to an exceptional degree." A defendant's desire for drug rehabilitation has also been considered as a permissible factor warranting a downward departure by the sentencing court. *United States v. Whitaker*, 152 F.3d 1238, 1240-41 (10th Cir. 1998).[13] Now that the Guidelines are merely advisory, these factors are relevant in determining a reasonable sentencing after *Booker* under §3553(a).[14]
15. The Defendant completely accepts responsibility for his conduct in this case. Today, the Defendant stands before this Court humbled, remorseful, and contrite. The Defendant recognizes that his conduct was wrong. The Defendant stands before this Court ashamed for his conduct, and ashamed that he has caused harm to others. The Defendant desperately wants to achieve a total rehabilitation so that he never again becomes involved in this type of conduct again. The Defendant's remorse is reflected in his acceptance of personal responsibility.
16. The Defendant's remorse and rehabilitation become even more relevant when coupled with the Defendant's age at the time of any

---

[12] *U.S. v. Fagan*, 162 F.3d 1280, 1284-85 (10th Cir. 1998).
[13] *U.S. v. Whitaker*, 152 F.3d 1238, 1240-41 (10th Cir. 1998).
[14] 18 U.S.C.A. §3553(a).

future release, making it extremely unlikely that the Defendant will commit other crimes in the future. The Defendant is currently fifty-four years old. After *Booker*, many courts have considered a defendant's age as a factor for sentencing below the Guidelines. *See Simon v. United States*, 361 F. Supp.2d 35, 48 (E.D.N.Y. 2005);[15] *United States v. Thomas*, 360 F.Supp.2d 238, 243 (D. Mass. 2005).[16] Further, according to the Sentencing Commission, "Recidivism rates decline relatively consistently as age increases," from 35.5 percent under age twenty-one, to 9.5 percent over age fifty, lessening the need to protect the public from further crimes of the defendant under 3553(a)(2)(C).[17] *See US Sentencing Commission, Measuring Recidivism: The Criminal History Computation of the Federal Sentencing Guidelines.* Thus, it is extremely unlikely that the Defendant will commit another crime should he be released.

17. Accordingly, the Defendant respectfully asks that this Court take these factors into consideration under §3553(a) in determining a sentence that is no greater than necessary.

2. <u>The Defendant's Substance Abuse History</u>

18. The Defendant has a long history of drug and alcohol use. The Defendant submits that he started consuming alcohol at the age of seventeen, and at times has used alcohol daily. (PSR at ¶76.) By the age of twenty-one, the Defendant was using cocaine and heroin, which was sometimes a daily habit. (PSR at ¶76.) At the time of his arrest in the instant matter, the Defendant was using heroin daily. (PSR at ¶75.)

CONCLUSION

19. The Defendant respectfully requests that the Court make factual findings and conclusions regarding each of the above arguments. Further, the Defendant submits that the Guidelines range in this case is greater than necessary to achieve the goals of sentencing under 18

---

[15] *Simon v. U.S.*, 361 F. Supp. 2d 35, 48 (E.D. N.Y. 2005).
[16] *U.S. v. Thomas*, 360 F. Supp. 2d 238, 243 (D. Mass. 2005).
[17] 18 U.S.C.A. §3553(a)(2)(C).

U.S.C. §3553(a).[18] Accordingly, the Defendant respectfully requests that this Court take into consideration the above factors and sentence the Defendant to the lowest term sufficient to achieve the goals of sentencing under §3553(a)(2).[19]

Pre-Sentence Motions

If you are convicted following trial, there could exist grounds to file a motion challenging the conviction before you are sentenced. In New York, a motion can be filed on any ground that would warrant a reversal or modification of the verdict on appeal. Additional grounds include juror misconduct and newly discovered evidence. These motions are rarely granted, but they often serve a greater purpose: they are a means of bringing to the judge's attention reasons warranting a lenient sentence, and they can help preserve important issues for a later appeal. It is ultimately up to your attorney whether to bring such a motion, but you should ask your attorney for his or her opinion on same.

Sentencing

By the time your sentencing date has arrived, the sentencing judge, or his law clerk, will already have reviewed everything you submitted, and the judge will have a pretty good idea of what his or her sentence will be. The reality is that nothing you or your attorney says during sentencing is likely to have a significant effect on the outcome. That does not mean there is nothing further you can do to help yourself at sentencing. Sometimes, the sentencing judge has only decided upon a certain range of sentences in his or her mind and is waiting to hear what you and/or your attorney has to say at sentencing before making a final decision.

The advice I gave regarding your appearance at the pre-sentence interview applies equally here. You should dress formally and appear respectful and contrite. I also strongly recommend that you have as many friends and family members as possible attend sentencing as a show of support. I like to introduce those in attendance to the judge during

[18] 18 U.S.C.A. §3553(a).
[19] 18 U.S.C.A. §3553(a)(2).

sentencing. That said, I also encourage you to speak with anyone planning to attend your sentencing beforehand to ask them to remain calm and quiet during sentencing. The prospect of hearing a judge send your son or daughter away to jail is, understandably, a very traumatizing event, and emotions are likely to run high. But you do not want an intimidating mob scene inside the courtroom caused by family members and friends losing their cool when they believe the judge has sentenced you too harshly. It can have no positive effect, and it is likely to only make things harder on you. It could also result in the judge holding those responsible for causing the scene in contempt of court, which can carry with it jail time.

Before you are sentenced, both your attorney and you have the right to speak directly to the judge. I recommend that you take advantage of the opportunity. There are two ways of doing so. Either you can speak "off the cuff," so to speak, or you can read something already prepared. It all really depends on your level of comfort. Even if you are comfortable speaking in public, I recommend that you at least bring with you some pre-prepared notes or an outline. Do not underestimate the stress and emotions you are likely to experience. Trying to remember everything you want to share with the judge under that stress and with those emotions is difficult, and you will likely forget important things. Whatever method you choose, just make sure whatever you say, it comes from your heart and it is said using your words. Nothing screams insincerity more than reciting or reading something prepared by your attorney or, for that matter, anyone who is not you. The judge wants to hear from you, not your attorney.

Some tips:

1. Do not complain about your attorney, how you were railroaded, the unfairness of the criminal justice system, the food in the jail, or any other matter. Do not complain.
2. Do not accuse the judge or prosecutor of treating you unfairly.
3. Do not plead your innocence. This is probably the trickiest issue you will have to deal with if you choose to speak at your sentencing. While you do not have to admit guilt if you really

believe you are not guilty, by telling the judge you did not do it, and you were wrongfully convicted, the judge is more likely to take that as a sign you are unremorseful and have not yet accepted responsibility for your actions than to actually believe you were wrongfully convicted. The best plan of attack is to simply say you respect the jury's verdict and leave it at that. Better to let your attorney deal with the issue of actual innocence in any pre-sentencing motions/submissions he or she might file or during sentencing when your attorney has an opportunity to speak. You have to remember that the judge heard and saw everything the jury heard and saw. Any doubt the judge may have regarding whether the jury got its verdict right will exist regardless of what you might say, and the judge will respect you more for taking the high road.

4. Refer to the judge as "your honor," "judge," or "sir" or "ma'am" when speaking.
5. Look the judge in the eyes when speaking.
6. Thank the judge for protecting your right to receive a fair trial.
7. If the sentence you will receive must include jail time, tell the judge how you will use the time in jail to have a positive effect on you. For example, you might plan to obtain your GED or undergo treatment for any drug and/or alcohol problems.
8. Show remorse to any victims. This one is related to tip number three. Unless you truly know or believe you did nothing wrong, showing genuine remorse to those you have hurt is important. For example, if you were convicted of assault, apologize to the person you assaulted.
9. Do not glare at anyone inside the courtroom, especially the judge, prosecutor, victim, or family and friends of the victim.

These tips are not exhaustive. You should discuss what you plan to say with your attorney before sentencing. If you have written anything down, you should have your attorney review it before sentencing.

By the time your sentencing date arrives, you should understand the possible sentences you face, including the likelihood of serving jail time. Certain crimes require either local jail time or time in state or federal prison. Understanding the likelihood of serving time in jail will allow you to prepare yourself both mentally and physically, including making proper arrangements for the care of your family and your finances. If you have been convicted of a felony offense following a trial, the likelihood of serving jail time is high. And if you are sentenced to serve time in jail, you will likely be taken into custody the moment the judge announces your sentence. Your attorney can request that the judge grant you what is known as a furlough, which is an additional amount of time to spend outside of custody before beginning serving your sentence, but furloughs are rarely granted. If a furlough is granted, the judge can elect to either schedule another court date for your surrender or schedule a date for your self-surrender directly at the institution where you will begin serving your sentence.

You should also let your family know that, if you are taken into custody, there will likely be a period of time, sometimes as much as a month, wherein you will not be allowed any outside contact. For instance, in New York, when beginning a state prison sentence, prisoners are sent to certain institutions for processing initially before being sent on to a permanent facility. Defendants serving state prison time arising from convictions in western New York are usually sent to Elmira Correctional Facility for approximately three weeks for processing. The period of time it takes to move prisoners from the local jail to a state or federal facility varies. You could be transferred within a day or it could take weeks, depending on numerous unpredictable factors, including the availability of transportation and space.

If jail time is possible as part of your sentence, you should ask your attorney to let you know if there are any programs that can act to shorten the amount of time you serve. Many such programs must be requested by you before the judge will consider them. For example, many states, such as New York, have drug and alcohol treatment programs that, if ordered by the court, can reduce your sentence to as short as ninety days. In New York, defendants convicted of a felony that is not a class A or B felony and is not a violent felony are eligible for the Willard Drug Treatment Program. If you were admitted into that program, you would serve ninety days in the program and, upon successful completion, be released from custody on parole.

Many states, such as New York, also have what are known as shock camp programs that can be ordered by the court upon the defendant's request. Shock camps are intensive boot camp-like programs that involve rigorous physical activity. In New York, for instance, the shock program runs for six months. Upon completion of the program, you are released from custody on parole. Thus, if you are eligible and admitted into the program, you can potentially reduce an otherwise longer sentence to six months.

In addition to jail time, sentences may also includes monetary penalties, including fines, surcharges, and restitution, where applicable. Restitution can be ordered by the judge when there exists a victim who has suffered some financial loss. Possible losses can include the loss of or damage to property and the cost of medical care. Where monetary penalties are ordered by the judge, you have some options for payment. Typically, defendants about to serve significant jail time request that the judge convert the amount owed to a civil judgment and order that collection be deferred until after the defendant is released. Whether to grant the request is left to the judge's discretion.

The advantage of this is that it usually prevents the penal institution from taking money out of your commissary account to pay the amount you owe. The primary disadvantage is that your credit will be negatively affected. If you or your family has the financial means to pay what is owed, your best option is to simply pay it and avoid a judgment. If you do not pay it voluntarily, however, any money deposited into your commissary account or earned by you while in jail could be taken by the facility to satisfy the debt.

Appeal

If all else fails, your final hope is to appeal your conviction to a higher court and seek to have the verdict reversed. Your right to appeal begins the moment you are sentenced. In New York, after you are sentenced, you have thirty days to file a notice of appeal. The notice of appeal is a written document that puts all the required parties on notice of your intention to appeal the verdict. It is your attorney's obligation to prepare and file a notice of appeal upon your request. Thus, as soon as you are convicted, you should notify your attorney orally and in writing that you wish to appeal the verdict. I recommend that you mail your attorney a letter before sentencing requesting that he or she prepare and file the notice of appeal.

The notice of appeal only begins the appeal process. Unless you hired your attorney, and an appeal was included in your attorney's scope of services, you will either need to hire an attorney to handle the appeal or request that the court appoint one to represent you. The process is complicated and lengthy, and I do not recommend that you try to handle the appeal yourself. After the notice of appeal is filed, a compilation of documents called the record on appeal must be prepared, followed by a brief setting forth all the grounds for your appeal. After everything required is filed, the appeal is argued orally before the court hearing the appeal.

Afterword

"Guilty." That was all I heard. And I hear it many nights when I lay awake, haunted by all of the verdicts that have eluded me in my career. I have been fortunate. I have managed to win many more than I have lost. But no matter how many successes I have enjoyed, it is the failures I remember the best. And this one stands at the top of the list, because I believed, and continue to believe, strongly in my client's innocence.

I do not look my client directly in the eye. Rather, I watch for his reaction from the corner of my eye, where I also see his wife, family, and friends display reactions ranging from shock to anger. I try to offer my hand by touching his shoulder, but I remain frozen in time, ashamed and self-conscious, feeling the stares of the jurors, judge, stenographer, and prosecutor, without really knowing whether it is real or imaginary.

I barely hear the judge ask me whether I want the jury polled, and I am not sure if he heard me say "No," but I assume he did as the judge next asked the assistant district attorney whether he wished to be heard on the issue of custody while we await a sentencing date. The assistant district attorney chooses not to kick me while I am down and defers to the court on the issue. I next give as compelling an argument as I can muster as to why John should not be taken into custody, pointing to the supportive gallery as I do. The judge also takes mercy on me, and more importantly John, ordering that John remain free while he awaits sentencing. The judge then reads what are referred to as Parker warnings in New York, warning John that if he fails to show up for sentencing, the judge can choose to proceed with sentencing him anyway.

After it is all over, I look at John directly for the first time. He returns the look and thanks me, tears in his eyes. I walk over to my adversary, the assistant district attorney, shake his hand, and congratulate him. We both know this likely will not be the last time we will square off inside the courtroom, just as it was not the first. He returns my graciousness, and I also thank the judge and his staff for their efforts and courtesies during the trial. You spend a lot of time with those who work inside a courtroom during a trial, and its conclusion always feels a little like saying goodbyes to the friends you made at summer camp.

By the time I walk outside the courtroom, John is huddling with his wife and family, consoling each other. I slide over, without inserting myself into the huddle, and tell John and his wife to go home, rest, and call me the following morning to chat. Emotions are high, and it makes no sense to attempt having any meaningful discussion now. There will be plenty of time for Monday morning quarterbacking tomorrow.

I leave the group behind and take the stairs down to the lobby rather than wait awkwardly for the next elevator. When I reach the lobby and leave the building, the Hall of Justice, my heart feels anything but justice. The fading day's natural light hits my face for the first time since lunchtime, and I walk alone down the sidewalk, the moment still feeling too surreal to attempt to make any sense of what just happened. I can barely feel my legs, and if I did not notice the courthouse getting further and further away as I walked, I would not have believed I was actually moving. I am walking with no real purpose, as both my car and office remain in the opposite direction.

I briefly consider turning around and waiting for the jurors to leave the courthouse so I can speak with them and ask where it went wrong, how I failed to raise even one reasonable doubt in their minds regarding John's guilt. I have done it before. It is permissible and a great opportunity to obtain professional critique and sometimes information that may give the defendant some degree of closure. But ultimately I decide against it and continue walking. I am simply too angry, and I fear I could take that anger out on the men and women who are the source of my anger. It is much easier to blame them than myself, because to blame myself would be to acknowledge there was something I could have done that would have changed the outcome.

My mobile phone rings, rather vibrates, as I have not yet taken it out of silent mode. I look at it to see it is my wife calling. I consider ignoring it, not yet ready to face anyone. But I hit the phone's accept button, hearing the small voices of my four- and five-year-old sons. Having no concept of how their dad is feeling or what he has done, they ask if I will be bringing them home a surprise today. And when the call is complete, I check my calendar, and I realize I begin my next trial in three weeks.

Frequently Asked Questions

Q. How long does a criminal case last?

A. The length of the typical felony criminal case depends on numerous factors, such as which court the case is in, the number of defendants, whether expert witnesses are expected to be called to testify at trial, the schedules of the defendant's attorney, prosecutor and judge, the complexity of the factual and legal issues involved and the number of witnesses expected to be called to testify, to name a few. That all said, the average case, from arraignment following indictment to trial generally takes about six months. In that six months, you should expect to make at least five court appearances, not including trial.

Q. How much does it cost to hire a private attorney?

A. This too depends on numerous factors, such as the seriousness of the crime and the court your case is in. Generally speaking, the more serious the crime, the more you are going to pay. You should also expect to pay more in bigger counties and expect to pay more in federal court than state court. For example, a private attorney in New York City is going to charge at least twice as much as an attorney in Upstate New York. In my home county of Monroe County, most private attorneys charge flat fees, while a few bill hourly. For a first time misdemeanor DWI in Monroe and the surrounding counties, you should expect to pay between $1,500 and $3,500, on average. Felony DWIs, on average, range from $3,000 to $10,000. Class B and C felonies range, on average, from $4,000 to $10,000. Class A felonies range, on average, from $5,000 to $20,000.

Q How often should I expect my attorney to visit me if I am in custody during my case?

A. I have found that lack of sufficient communication is the number one grievance among defendants against their attorneys. This is particularly true for defendants in custody. I can understand it. Your client is locked up in a building without ears or eyes to monitor what is going on with his or her case. Telephone calls are either prohibited or severely restricted. Mail is scrutinized closely by jail officials and seems to take twice as long to arrive at its intended destination than normal mail. Defendants are constantly barraged with the talk of "jail-house lawyers" enhancing their anxiety by whispering things like: "Your lawyer doesn't know what he is doing", "Why didn't your lawyer file this motion?" or "Why didn't your lawyer get you a lower bail?" It is easy to understand how a defendant can feel helpless and forgotten, even by his own attorney.

Unfortunately, if you hired a good lawyer, you also hired a busy lawyer, which means your lawyer must find time to visit probably fifty or more clients, while still committing the necessary time to being in the courtroom, writing motions and researching law. It is simply not practical to expect your attorney to visit you in custody more than once per month, unless there is an emergency or some other extenuating circumstance. That said, your attorney should be expected to keep you regularly apprised of the status of your case though writing letters or contacting you on the telephone, where allowed. If you write your attorney a letter, it is not asking too much to expect a response within a week of receipt.

Q. If I fire my attorney before the case is over, am I entitled to get any money back?

A. Yes. In New York, there is no such thing as earned upon receipt. In other words, if you pay your attorney the requested $2,500 on Monday and fire him Tuesday, he cannot keep $2,500. In New

York, when terminated prior to completion of the agreed-upon services, an attorney is only entitled to keep the reasonable value of the services actually rendered. Most written retainer agreements, including the example contained herein, provide that the attorney may bill for his time spent up to termination at his normal hourly rate. That hourly rate can sometimes be negotiated with the attorney when hiring him or her–the lower the hourly rate, the more you are likely to get refunded should you decide to terminate the attorney.

Q. If I am in custody during my case, and the court has already set bail or is holding me without any bail, can my attorney ask the court again to release me or lower my bail?

A. You only get one bite at the apple unless there has been a "material change in circumstances" since the first bail application. What that means is, once your attorney has made an application on your behalf for bail, he or she cannot do so again unless something significant has changed since that application. One change of circumstances warranting a new application is newly discovered favorable evidence, like a key witness for the prosecution retracting his or her statement to the police.

Q. If I am convicted, who handles my appeal?

A. In New York state court, the attorney that handled your case is not obligated to also handle your appeal. If you are represented by a private attorney, you can either hire that attorney to also handle your appeal or hire a new attorney for the appeal. If you were represented by a public defender, an attorney from the public defender's office specializing in appeals will usually handle the appeal, unless you hire a private attorney. There are attorneys that specialize in doing appeals. If you can afford to hire an attorney for your appeal, I recommend that you hire an attorney that specializes in appeals. In federal court, the attorney that represented you during the case is obligated to also handle your appeal unless you terminate him or her and hire a new attorney for the appeal.

ABOUT THE AUTHOR

Kevin McKain has represented criminal defendants in both state and federal court for over a decade, as well as serving on the other side of the criminal case as a special prosecutor. Mr. McKain has taken over fifty cases to trial, including more than thirty jury trials, and has represented defendants accused of everything from DWI to murder.

ASPATORE